The Art of Appraisal

The Art of Appraisal

Effective Tools and Streamlined Processes to Boost Teacher Performance

Barbara D. Culp

ROWMAN & LITTLEFIELD
Lanham • Boulder • New York • London

Published by Rowman & Littlefield
A wholly owned subsidiary of
The Rowman & Littlefield Publishing Group, Inc.
4501 Forbes Boulevard, Suite 200, Lanham, Maryland 20706
https://rowman.com

Unit A, Whitacre Mews, 26-34 Stannary Street, London SE11 4AB,
United Kingdom

Copyright © 2017 by Barbara D. Culp

All rights reserved. No part of this book may be reproduced in any form or by any electronic or mechanical means, including information storage and retrieval systems, without written permission from the publisher, except by a reviewer who may quote passages in a review.

British Library Cataloguing in Publication Information Available

Library of Congress Cataloging-in-Publication Data

Includes bibliographic references.
ISBN 978-1-4758-3764-3 (cloth : alk. paper)
ISBN 978-1-4758-3765-0 (pbk. : alk. paper)
ISBN 978-1-4758-3766-7 (Electronic)

∞ ™ The paper used in this publication meets the minimum requirements of American National Standard for Information Sciences Permanence of Paper for Printed Library Materials, ANSI/NISO Z39.48-1992.

Printed in the United States of America

Nine tenths of education is encouragement.

—Anatole France

Contents

Foreword ix
Preface xi
Acknowledgments xv
Introduction xvii

I: Preparation
1 Looking Back 3
2 Parsing Performance 7

II: Ten Key Responsibilities
3 Laying the Foundation 17
4 Professionalism 25
5 Planning and Preparation 35
6 Classroom Management 45
7 Teaching with Rigor 53
8 Teamsmanship 61
9 Administrative Duties 71
10 Instruction 79
11 Pastoral Duties 87
12 Behavioral Competencies 95
13 Teacher as Leader 103

III: Preformed Comments
14 Useful Comments   113
15 Performance Tier Words and Phrases   135

About the Author   141

Foreword

Teacher evaluation has always been a controversial topic in the educational arena. Stephen Sawchuk defines teacher evaluation as a school's official process for assessing and ranking performance and effectiveness. He notes that evaluations should ideally yield both feedback and developmental guidance.

In recent years, evaluation has become more prevalent as the pressures to improve our educational system have mounted. These programs have themselves undergone many changes. The major factors that have propelled these movements are new research on teacher quality, philanthropic grants to improve teacher effectiveness, advocacy groups, political pressure to fire poorly performing teachers, and state takeover of low-performing schools.

In the 2000s, researchers began to deeply analyze student test data. They found that the students of effective teachers consistently performed significantly higher than others. Stanford University economist Eric A. Hanushek estimated that top teachers helped students gain more than a grade's worth of learning. Students taught by the lowest performers achieved only half a year of learning.

During that same time frame, the Bill and Melinda Gates Foundation focused on teacher evaluation. Approximately $700 million was designated for teacher quality and initiatives, much of which was dedicated to attempts to implement improved evaluation systems in a handful of districts. Through the 2009 American Reinvestment and Recovery Act, the federal government provided $4.3 million for this same effort. The Department of Education initiated the Race to the Top, which offered grants to states that agreed to change their policies and develop and implement new evaluation systems.

Advocacy groups, meanwhile, constantly call for ineffective teachers and teachers whose students perform poorly on tests to be eliminated. Our present evaluation system, they contend, is not working. They constantly compare the school to a business and demand that the same model apply to both.

Politicians have long campaigned with promises to improve schools. The interpretation of this overwhelmingly has been dismissal of poorly performing teachers. To take this step, a solid teacher-evaluation system must be in place and used effectively.

The importance of this effort is seen in the significant interest in state takeovers of poorly performing schools. In some districts, the state actually has taken this step. One of the main components of the process has been to implement stronger teacher-evaluation systems. In a different trend, poorly performing schools are assigned to private companies that seem to more easily evaluate and remove poor performers.

Regardless of who runs the school or district, one thing is clear: a strong evaluation system must be in place, and the administrator must use it so the schools can be successful.

A preponderance of evidence proves that teacher evaluation is a major component of effective schools. Administrators must embrace the idea and seek fair and productive ways to evaluate teachers, using appropriate criteria and instruments. Assessment is a time-consuming task, but a crucial one. Administrators cannot consider evaluation a perfunctory, low-priority task.

The Art of Appraisal provides a blueprint that will assist administrators in making good teachers great, average teachers good, and poor teachers average or better. If necessary, this blueprint will help them eliminate teachers who continue to perform at low levels. The charts included in the last few chapters are a particularly valuable tool.

The author, Dr. Barbara D. Culp, has over forty years of experience in public education as a classroom teacher, a principal, and a resource for principals. She has been in the trenches, so she knows the importance of evaluations as well as the productive use of time. I commend her for sharing her expertise, and I only wish that I had been given this reference when I started my career.

Dr. Jacquelyn S. Daniel, Former Executive Director of
Curriculum and Instruction, Georgia

Preface

For over forty years, my efforts as an educational professional persevered through shrinking resources and increasing demands. Like you, I was asked to provide our children with a quality education despite cutbacks and constant change. One tool was a reliable and constant source of school-wide improvement: the appraisal.

Richly detailed and meaningful feedback helps teachers to thrive. An appraisal can provide this, and so much more. And yet the entire process, from finding time for class visits to creating effective feedback, presents challenges.

Visits must be performed for every classroom, and yet the usual administrative workload can't be put on pause. The appraisal comments must address instructional methods and student behavior. The individual preferences and methodologies that impact teaching and learning must be addressed in a comprehensive and consistent manner.

This demanding task must be applied fairly and effectively across the entire spectrum of professional ability. Every teacher must receive individualized feedback that is specific and practical. At every step in the evaluation process, administrators must be conscious of and able to manage a number of diverse tasks and needs.

All this means that the appraisal process takes time, and yet time is the one resource that is always at a premium in our districts. The administration's approach to how evaluations are implemented therefore needs to be manageable and efficient. To be effective, the results must provide meaningful feedback that lifts educators and, by extension, the classrooms they serve.

I was certain that evaluations could be provided in a way that is efficient, productive, and easy for everyone involved. More than that, I felt that the process had to live up to its potential. The intent behind appraisals is valid, after all, and the goal for every evaluation is to generate a richly productive academic atmosphere in which students and teachers can succeed.

After writing five different books for educational professionals, parents, and students, I turned my attention to the critical tool of teacher appraisals. I developed a streamlined approach that generates meaningful, actionable comments. The book you're holding in your hands distills decades of real-world experience as a teacher, principal, clinical supervisor, tutor, and parent into a very compact handful of chapters. Using this book, you'll discover the best path forward so that you, your teachers, and your school will reap the maximum benefits.

Speaking on a personal level, I hope that you will discover that *The Art of Appraisal* is much more than a tool. It's a method that will hone your administrative skills and leadership abilities so you can achieve everything demanded of you . . . and then go on to achieve even more. The process honors the very real impact teachers have on our children, our schools, and our communities. I hope that you will accept and use this gift to lift your school to ever greater success.

During my tenure in Georgia's public schools, I learned one very important thing: everyone counts. The parents who trust your school enough to send their children into its classrooms count. The personnel who manage the myriad details that carry your school through every hour of the day and every day of the academic year count. The students who arrive from every walk of life count.

Most of all, our teachers count. They pour their sweat and laughter and even tears into their lesson plans. They are shepherds for the young minds that will one day leave the school's pasture and head out on their own. For part of every day, teachers are surrogate parents and taskmasters, leaders and companions. Theirs are the hands that implement the tasks and duties you hand down.

And they need you. Teachers need your expertise and experience. They look to you for guidance and assistance. At every milestone in the academic year and during the periods in between, they need to hear from you that they are on target. They need to be told that their efforts are paying off for the students and the school. The appraisal process might be official, but it is also an opportunity to connect, commend, and communicate.

Nothing is more powerful than the human touch. Nothing will spur your educational professionals to higher levels than your feedback, assistance, and approval. Because this element is critical to continued success, this more personal aspect has been integrated into *The Art of Appraisal*. The book's final chapters provide long lists of preformed comments you can use to quickly generate rich and insightful feedback.

Today, we have the benefit of looking back across centuries of school history. We can see how appraisals arose, track their refinement over the decades, and understand how the process can enhance education. We also have the ability to recognize that, although methodologies might differ, the final goal is always academic excellence.

Just as we treat students as individuals who bring their own beliefs, attitudes, and opinions to their learning, you can treat teaches as individuals with their own preferences. No one person's management of his or her classroom will look exactly like a different person's approach. Honoring those preferences while offering valuable recommendations is the best path forward.

Providing appraisals—effective, detailed evaluations with rich and useful recommendations—truly is an art. The steps that take you from start to finish must be easy to implement, and they must efficiently mesh with all your other duties. Both feedback and developmental guidance must be the end result, and those results must be achieved in a compassionate and caring manner.

The Art of Appraisal is your road map to exactly that type of success. When a strong evaluation system is in place, schools can be wildly successful. Graduates of sterling schools bring the knowledge and maturity developed through their education to their communities. In this way, every gift of effort, hope, and love offered by you and your teachers is also given to your community as well as to our society.

I hope that you will accept *The Art of Appraisal* in the spirit in which it is truly given: as a gift for you, your teachers, and everyone involved with your school.

Acknowledgments

I wish to acknowledge the support of my longtime friend Laine Cunningham. She has walked beside me on this journey for at least ten years, teaching and grooming me for successful publication. She helped me fine-tune and express my ideas in ways that encouraged an editor to take a chance on me.

She was there when writing made me beam with excitement as well as when I was depressed by the whole idea and ready to give up. Every time, she always offered the right words to rekindle my desire to keep going. In addition, she has the innate ability to sense passion in others, and she drives them to explore and never give up. During our journey, she brought me to the door of success. All I had to do was knock, and Rowman & Littlefield Publishing answered.

Laine is an accomplished writer in her own right, with countless books to her credit, along with several ghostwritten works. To my friend, I wish you continued success in all your endeavors. Know that I would not be the author I am today if it were not for you. Love you always!

Introduction

Hands down, teacher evaluations are one of the most useful tools available to principals. In addition to identifying an educator's strengths, a thoughtful approach pinpoints areas where a teacher can improve. With the addition of a few detailed comments, an appraisal can correct weak habits, boost the performance of midlevel professionals, and propel excellent teachers into greatness.

To achieve maximum benefits, the individuals who receive the appraisals have to trust that they provide value. Much of that trust is going to be triggered by the principal's attitude toward the process. Even administrators who recognize how important appraisals are might undermine their results because evaluations take so much time . . . and time is one resource principals need to manage down to the minute.

In addition to allowing for smooth implementation, the appraisal process needs to result in accurate and meaningful feedback. To realize the fullness of this potential impact, the comments must include recommendations that can be utilized in the classroom. Sterling professionals, midlevel teachers, and low performers alike should receive feedback that guides them toward better practices.

To ensure that every moment spent on appraisals produces consistent, measurable improvement, think of the feedback as a binary element. All appraisals should point out (1) strengths and (2) weaknesses. Each of these two categories can then be subdivided into specific areas that connect with state and federal mandates, the unique needs of a specific school's population, and the place where every teacher stands in her or his development.

During my forty-plus years of working as an educational professional, I have seen firsthand the shrinking resources and increasing demands placed on every level of our system. Year after year, the professionals who teach our nation's children have been asked to do more and more with less and less. The art of appraisal, the ability to provide richly detailed and meaningful feedback, has never been more important than it is today.

And yet using this tool is challenging. You step into a classroom for one visit knowing that, day by day, student-teacher interactions and the methods of teaching will change. The level of engagement by students might be impacted by events in the school or the community. The teachers and paraprofessionals are dealing with personal and other issues that might temporarily impact their performance in the classroom.

Into this mix, you will inject your opinions about teaching methods, student behavior, and even your understanding of different personalities. The task is demanding. Nevertheless, you must focus on indicators of performance, record them accurately, and provide comments that constructively improve individual classrooms.

Your efforts must be applied across the entire spectrum of ability displayed by educational professionals at your school. Research indicates that very few teachers inside our educational system function at a low performance level. As much as 90 percent fall into the middle realm.[1] If your appraisals focus on only the few who are at the bottom, neither your school nor your students will benefit.

Every teacher therefore needs individualized feedback. Comments made in an appraisal must be specific and practical. Even recommendations that need time to implement should be accessible using the resources available to your school. Only then will the proper support be provided so that student learning can be enhanced.

The Art of Appraisal ensures that both the process and the results are efficient, effective, and productive. This book streamlines the approach and provides meaningful, actionable comments that can enhance the performance of those average performers and lift your entire school. Teachers in need of more assistance will find that their performance can change significantly. Even your top-tier educators will benefit.

In this book, you'll learn how and why appraisals started and, importantly, why appraisals might fail to reach their lofty goals. Utilizing this broad understanding, you'll turn to the process. A binary approach simplifies the procedure while allowing for rich, detailed, and meaningful feedback that will push your school to a higher rung of achievement.

Four rating tiers will be defined in a way that provides an overall perspective on performance. Ten critical areas for which every pre-K through 12 teacher is responsible will be defined. Each of these areas will be broken out into four subcategories to ensure that the appraisal is comprehensive. In every case, real examples will enhance your insight and cement your understanding.

In the final section, lists of specific comments and keywords and phrases are provided. These recommendations are laid out so they connect with each of the key responsibilities targeted in the streamlined approach. Most can be used without modification. In cases when you want to make an adjustment, you'll need to change only a few words or add a short phrase to tailor the comment to a specific teacher, mandate, or issue.

Providing appraisals really is an art. It relies foremost on your experience as a professional and your ability to locate the strengths and weaknesses of each educator in your school. But that doesn't mean appraisals have to be a burden. Like painters who use premixed tubes of color, you can create a rich and insightful appraisal with the comments, feedback, and recommendations compiled in *The Art of Appraisal.*

NOTE

1. "Seeing It Clearly: Improving Observer Training for Better Feedback and Better Teaching." The Bill and Melinda Gates Foundation, August 2015.

I

Preparation

Chapter One

Looking Back

Teacher appraisals evolved from two very different arenas.

First was the education system, which at its inception was entirely focused on religious knowledge. Academic achievement was restricted to reading, and that skill was taught only so individuals could benefit from reading the Bible. The other area that impacted appraisals was the growth of industry in various economic sectors.

Once the benefits of a formal appraisal process were realized, schools adopted the process for their teachers. By delving into the history of different evaluations, an interesting perspective is gained on the system of appraisals applied to today's educational professionals.

DEVELOPMENT OF APPRAISALS

In the seventeenth century, the first schools opened in the British North Atlantic colonies. Rather than placing a fully rounded education at the heart of their mission, these institutions were driven by specific missions. They strove only to teach boys how to read so their spiritual growth could be enhanced by engaging with the Bible's written words.

Not surprisingly, members of the clergy were considered the best individuals to place in teaching positions. Local governments provided the necessary funds and laid out specifications for the curriculum. Any textbooks that might be needed were imported from England.[1]

Right from the beginning, then, teachers were first and foremost in service to their community. Individual supervisors or supervisory committees were created by the community to monitor the teachers' effectiveness. The type of feedback provided and the elements on which they were judged varied quite a bit from one community to the next. Both the job and the evaluation of that job were as unique as the village or town.

During the next century, schools began accepting all the children from the community. Parents whose children attended school paid special fees that were added to the government funds. Different grade levels were taught in a single room by a single instructor. The curriculum was limited and primarily covered basic reading and math skills. Except for a few places in the northern states, teaching slaves or their children was illegal.

By that point, clergy were no longer considered the optimal instructors. The jobs fell instead to several women who needed to support themselves. Even among men who took on the role, teaching was considered a temporary occupation until marriage or a position in a career field opened. Formal credentials were not required. In fact, few teachers held more education than what they provided to the children.

In the early nineteenth century, industrialization and the demand for a standardized curriculum spurred the creation of two-year teaching colleges.[2] Large schools and districts hired multiple experts in a variety of subjects. As the operation of schools became increasingly complex, a single teacher was often assigned administrative duties. The head teacher, also called the principal teacher, eventually became the principal we know today.

As industrialized jobs became the norm, the way supervisors viewed workers—teachers included—changed. The salaries of machine workers and other laborers were increasingly tied to the quantity of finished material. After World War I, performance appraisals were implemented for a wide range of blue-collar jobs. Another few decades passed before appraisals were applied to white-collar positions.

Since appraisals could be manipulated by dishonest managers, the Civil Rights Act of 1964 and Equal Employment Opportunity Commission guidelines pressured companies to set up formalized processes. For teachers, this was good news. Their evaluations stopped focusing on their personality traits and instead considered only their skills. Evaluations also began to be applied in a more scientific manner.[3]

Unfortunately, the methodology was burdened with overly broad and cluttered lists of evaluation points. In the late 1950s, clinical supervision provided an innovative approach. By the mid-1980s, even the clinical approach was considered too restrictive. Developmental and reflective models were brought in to allow for diverse perspectives and greater flexibility. By the twenty-first century, appraisals had become much more like the process we see today.

IMPACT ON SCHOOLS

For a long span of time, unions have lobbied for teacher salaries and benefits to be tied to experience and training. This method seems fair and equitable, but those components are a very small part of the larger picture. The real yardstick of effectiveness is the level of academic excellence and growth that students display.

Recently, *Harvard Political Review* called the changes undergone by the appraisal system since 2009 "revolutionary."[4] Student achievement is now of paramount importance. The system has, however, caused some difficulties. Implementing evaluations and tracking the data they produce require effort. With administrations already stretched to their limits, as much time and effort as possible must be freed up to keep schools functioning.

A study by the University of Virginia indicates that the efforts involved with providing appraisals are worth the payoff. Under the old system, District of Columbia teachers who were rated at the highest and the lowest levels left at about the same rate. The new system, which utilizes multiple appraisals and feedback throughout the year, retained more high-achieving teachers.[5]

Importantly, the average turnover rates didn't change significantly. What did change was that lower-achieving staff left at higher rates than before. Under the old system, teacher turnover resulted in lower academic performance. In the new system, turnover was beneficial. It eliminated the lowest performers and replaced them with average or high performers.

As the quality of teachers rose, so did student achievement. On average, students' achievement rates in math and reading rose to a rate equal to four months of learning. The influx of better teachers also meant that when high-performing teachers did leave, the impact to the student body was significantly reduced.

Teacher appraisals, then, do more than enhance academic achievement. When feedback is fair, equitable, and useful, high performers stay at the school. Low performers often take the initiative and leave after their first poor score. Even when they hang on and must be dismissed, turnover allows better teachers to fill their positions. Turnover rates become a productive element of the school.

Finally, teachers rated as average or above average know that their contributions are appropriately valued. As individuals with issues are assisted through an appraisal's feedback, the school's teachers are surrounded by peers who are equally dedicated and capable. And as we all know, a positive work environment filled with like-minded coworkers is one of the best drivers of success.

CONCLUSION

Today, we have the benefit of looking back across centuries of appraisals in education as well as other fields. We can recognize what worked well, worked only partially, and failed miserably. The current system emphasizes the single point that most effectively relays a teacher's performance: academic excellence.[6]

Unfortunately, the spectrum of evaluation points can still feel overly broad and poorly categorized. This leads to a lot of confusion and, despite attempts to create a one-size program, appraisals can all too easily miss areas where a school, classroom, or teacher needs assistance.

It doesn't have to be that way. We can take the best and, using the modern model as our foundation, arrive at a clear, concise method that is easy to understand and just as easy to implement.

The past is the past. Today, appraisal is an art.

NOTES

1. Singer, Alan. "A Brief History of Education in the United States (Part 1)." The Huffington Post, September 7, 2015. Retrieved from http://www.huffingtonpost.com/alan-singer/welcome-back-a-brief-hist_b_8098916.html.

2. Compensation Café. "Where Did Performance Appraisals Come From?" May 14, 2012. Retrieved from http://www.compensationcafe.com/2012/05/where-did-performance-appraisals-come-from.html.

3. Ibid.

4. Rucinski, Melanie and Diersing, Colin. "America's Teacher Evaluation System Revolution." Harvard Political Review. May 14, 2014. Retrieved from http://harvardpolitics.com/united-states/americas-teacher-evaluation-system-revolution/.

5. Booren, Leslie M. "Study: Targeted Teacher Turnover Boosts Teacher Quality, Student Achievement." University of Virginia Today. January 26, 2016.

6. Marzano, Robert J., Frontier, Tony, and Livingston, David. "Effective Supervision." ASCD, 2011.

Chapter Two

Parsing Performance

Before you write any comments on the page, you must consider the level at which the teacher has performed. A four-tier ranking system provides an efficient process that is easy and effective. The four tiers also make things crystal clear for the person being appraised.

To understand the four tiers, think of performance in a binary fashion, with two baseline judgments: strength or weakness. If a teacher demonstrates strength in an area, one of the first two performance tiers will apply. The remaining tiers target areas where the educator is weak. Once you've determined whether an element is a strength or weakness, you can select from one of the two relevant tiers.

Taken together, the four tiers are:

- Excellent
- Satisfactory
- Needs Improvement
- Unsatisfactory

Each subsection in this chapter deals with an individual performance tier. Tips on judging performance and examples from actual appraisals ensure that you can quickly determine a teacher's performance level. Information in Part II will allow you to clearly communicate why her performance was assigned to a particular tier.

STRENGTHS

For strengths, consider whether the performance is Excellent or Satisfactory.

Satisfactory

Individuals who perform in a satisfactory method are proficient at that task. They have a foundational understanding of the task and can deliver in a way that meets state and federal mandates. Their actions are practical, and their methods result in expected levels of educational achievement.

Here is an example from an appraisal performed for a second-grade grammar workshop:

> The lesson appealed to students, was appropriate for the curriculum, and aligned to the goals of the lesson. It was a short lesson packed with good transferable information.

This teacher's performance was satisfactory because the lesson met the curricular objectives and provided useful, relevant information. Although the lesson was brief, it was geared to the classroom and appropriate for the age group.

The following example comes from an eighth-grade math session:

> I was very impressed with the details of your plan and your lesson delivery. You are a natural in the classroom! You planned comprehensively and provided materials and resources that were major contributors to students' ability to clearly understand the Pythagorean Theorem. The discussion and activities were conducted in a manner that allowed each student to build on his or her prior knowledge base.

The teacher received a satisfactory rating because the lesson plan met the requirements of the learning unit. The materials helped students grasp math concepts that can be confusing. Additionally, the unit utilized the foundation of knowledge built up during previous classes.

An eighth-grade chemistry unit yielded this comment:

> You clearly explained the lesson objective and communicated expectations for learning. The facts of the lesson were accurately presented. Restating key information helped students understand, and you clearly possess a rich knowledge of the topic.

Portions of this commentary focus on the teacher's own understanding of the subject matter, which was appropriate for the lesson. The way the teacher guided the students, by explaining objectives, communicating expectations, and rephrasing certain details, was also part of expected performance.

Excellent

An excellent rating applies to individuals who go above and beyond. Their understanding of a particular task is deeper than average, and their ability to implement that knowledge exceeds that expected of an average teacher. Their actions create the space and time students need to explore in new or more meaningful ways.

Here's an example from an appraisal for a social studies unit in which students rotated through five workstations to learn about the Middle East:

> By using your talent as an instructor to make standard material appealing and valid, you enhanced both engagement and comprehension. Materials were prearranged to help capitalize on the time allowed. You provided a brief overview of the station expectations. The rotations were smooth, and the nine minutes allowed for each station appeared to be sufficient for the activities. Students were attentive and wasted little time in pursuit of achieving each station's objective.

This teacher's performance met the usual expectations and then went beyond to achieve an excellent rating. This was accomplished by using textbook materials to create hands-on activities.

The interactive component consisted of several activities, each of which focused on a different aspect of the lesson. The stations had been prepared ahead of time to allow for full use of class time, and students were briefed on the purpose of each station before rotations began. All in all, this was a sterling example of performance at the highest level.

Here is an example from a fifth-grade science unit:

> You delivered an impressive lesson on inherited traits versus environmental characteristics! It was exciting and engaging. It was evident that a good deal of planning and preparation went into your lesson.
>
> Your use of real-life examples gave students an excellent insight into the main concept, and the PowerPoint presentation greatly enhanced the students' understanding. What a pleasure it was to observe a lesson provided with strong methods that inspired students to learn and generated a powerful academic environment.

This unit achieved the top tier for a variety of reasons. The planning that went into the lesson and the teacher's depth of understanding were both evident. The way the teacher communicated brought complex facts to life. By connecting the lesson to the world outside the classroom, the teacher built a bridge between academics and everyday life. The presentation tool fit the material and the readiness of the students. Because all these elements were brought to bear in the same lesson, the performance rank was clearly Excellent.

A third-grade math appraisal offers another look at excellent performance:

> You infused technology with the use of a PowerPoint presentation on division and multiplication. You used words of encouragement for student responses. You used diagrams and graphics to help students visualize the concept. I was glad to see the use of whole- and small-group instruction.
>
> You timed the activities and used a variety of strategies to achieve the lesson's objective. You were enthusiastic and taught a lesson that was hands-on, eyes on, and mind on. You owned the lesson from beginning to end.

In this case, the presentation tool allowed diagrams and graphics to highlight and clarify different points as they were discussed. The mixture of whole-class and group discussions switched between learning modes, which fostered engagement. Because the lesson implemented so many aspects of learning, this teacher excelled.

WEAKNESSES

In areas where a teacher displays weakness, his performance will be ranked either as Needs Improvement or Unsatisfactory.

Needs Improvement

Individuals who need improvement in an area do not possess all the foundational knowledge required to present lessons. Alternately, they might possess the knowledge but fail to implement what they know effectively. The benefits students receive are delivered sporadically, succeeding sometimes and failing at other times.

The teacher's performance is borderline, yet she can clearly become better if given guidance or training. Recognizing this element is critical. Needing assistance isn't the hallmark of a poor teacher or one who isn't properly motivated. It signals only that they aren't meeting expectations due to some weakness that can be remedied.

This example comes from a ninth-grade social studies unit:

> You appeared a little nervous at first; then you gained your confidence and the lesson took off. At this point, you should be writing your own plans or at least tweaking the standard plans to fit your teaching style. I would like to see you circulate the classroom more and call on more students to ensure that they are all with you.

The difficulties experienced in this classroom had multiple negative effects. A lack of confidence can encourage poor student behavior or fail to spark enthusiastic effort. Copying existing lesson plans didn't help the teacher grow and might have been related to low self-confidence. The lack of interaction and engagement between teacher and student further compounded these issues.

While the commentary addressed separate issues, all these difficulties could stem from a new teacher's lack of confidence in her abilities. Once she develops better leadership skills, she will engage students more directly, move confidently through the classroom, be more creative with lesson planning, and provide a strong launch for each lesson. It would be appropriate to discuss leadership skills with this teacher during follow-up sessions.

When a ninth-grade geography class used a game, a potentially powerful teaching tool failed to achieve even a satisfactory rating:

> Although the game kept students attentive, it didn't seem to have a relevant end. Perhaps clues or cue cards could be tied to the lesson's end.

This lesson was called out for guidance because the time spent on the game didn't provide an appropriate payoff. The steps of the game could have been tied into the lesson plan before the game began, during play, or after the game was finished. The failure to build the bridge between this activity and the curriculum resulted in a weaker performance rating.

This comment came from an appraisal for a kindergarten class that was mostly good but needed adjustment in one area:

> Art is a science. Please take some time to strengthen your skills. Students need vivid examples and good representation from visual aids.

In this lesson, the teacher was attempting to exhibit the differences between day and night. The selection of supportive materials needed to be done thoughtfully. The lack of understanding on the teacher's part led to less than optimal learning in the classroom, so the teacher needed to recognize his own deficit.

Unsatisfactory

Significant weaknesses fall on the unsatisfactory tier. This rank reflects foundational knowledge that is too undermined or spare to allow an educator to teach. The weakness might also come from a nearly complete inability to convey her knowledge in the classroom.

Individuals who perform at this level might lift their skills through specific development opportunities, but they must dedicate themselves to improvement if this is to be accomplished. Comments rated at this level should include recommendations for adjustments. These comments can be included in the appraisal or become part of the follow-up sessions.

An example from an elementary social studies unit reveals a clear need for further support:

> You have demonstrated that you can write comprehensive lesson plans and prepare activities that address the needs of all learners. The area that needs some attention is with consistently getting and maintaining students' attentive behaviors throughout your lessons.
>
> Today's observation was one of those lessons where students were not as cooperative as they should have been. Students' excitement about the lesson got the better of them. The lesson did not achieve its desired objective due to a failure to maintain students' full attention, resulting in too much playfulness and a lack of focus.

In this case, the teacher's ability to generate excitement and enthusiasm far outstripped the ability to control classroom behavior. The teacher captured attention at some points but was unable to do so consistently. Adding to that difficulty was the failure to maintain students' attention once it was focused on the lesson.

Because the teacher could generate such excitement with the lesson plan, he clearly had built the skills for preparation and academic depth. But none of that matters if chaos reigns inside the classroom. In this case, the individual must develop social and communication skills alongside leadership ability to achieve effectiveness.

This commentary comes from a third-grade science appraisal:

> Please work on becoming proficient with classroom technology. Also, establish the rules of engagement for hands-on lessons. Continue giving attention to classroom management strategies that work. Respond to disruptive behaviors in a timely manner and continue to work on strategies to better manage students' behaviors during class. Try using the Fairness Stick to call on students while keeping them alert and focused.

In this case, multiple observations were made over several months for the same teacher. Despite comments that repeatedly called out the same issues and offered recommendations, the teacher was not progressing in certain areas. This situation resulted in an Unsatisfactory rating.

During a kindergarten math unit, a major misstep was pinpointed in the appraisal:

> As a student teacher, you are not permitted to copy the Georgia Department of Education math frameworks as your lesson plans. Rather, you are expected to

> demonstrate skill in lesson planning by writing your own, using the framework and other sources as guides.

The student teacher was skating by with exact copies of the state's curriculum. Because the individual was in training, this action was egregious. The whole point of working in classrooms is to develop skills and take risks. Copying a plan was lazy and unproductive for her own learning goals. This did not bode well for when (or if) she eventually stepped into her role as a professional.

CONCLUSION

Keeping things simple generates an appraisal process that is highly efficient. When the pressures associated with time lines and limited resources are removed, the appraisals you provide automatically become more effective.

Keeping the approach simple also ensures that the comments, feedback, and thoughts in the appraisal are clear. Communication is key because teachers need to understand exactly where they shine and exactly how they can improve. Corralling responses into Excellent, Satisfactory, Needs Improvement, and Unsatisfactory provides exactly the type of information and feedback instructors need to excel.

The binary approach parses each area into a strength or a weakness. Setting only two tiers under each, your options range across four tiers. This very simple and direct ranking system is the basis for everything you'll do while providing appraisals. It's a rubric that serves everyone!

II

Ten Key Responsibilities

Chapter Three

Laying the Foundation

Depending on your existing approach to the appraisal process, you might be tracking hundreds of duties teachers must perform. These can range from very broad dictates, like enhancing academic excellence, down to the minutia involved in attendance rosters. Adding to this are the individual teaching preferences you'll appraise in classrooms that are run in very different ways.

As you move from one grade level to another, you'll be asked to evaluate the performance of teachers in charge of classrooms at different academic levels and with different learning needs. And it's only human to compare everyone to the exceptional performers, which means that the judgments applied to average performers might end up being too harsh.

In every case, you must approach each teacher as an independent professional. Each instructor must be judged on his own abilities and skills. He must not suffer in comparison to exceptional teachers, and the school can't afford for appraisals to be skewed high by comparisons to poor performances.

Trust me when I say that the management of all these elements is not impossible. In fact, by corralling the assessment points into related categories, those hundreds of different tasks boil down to ten key elements. These ten keys are:

- Professionalism
- Planning and preparation
- Classroom management
- Teaching with rigor
- Teamsmanship/spirit of cooperation
- Administrative duties
- Instruction

- Pastoral duties
- Core behavioral competencies
- Teacher as leader

These different areas of responsibility provide a comprehensive view of how well a teacher is fulfilling her expected assignments. By subdividing each of these ten responsibilities into four separate components, a seemingly overwhelming list is arranged into coherent areas. The appraisal process becomes logical, comprehensive, and meaningful.

Now, let's consider each key responsibility and its relevant subcategories. This chapter provides a brief introduction to each. More detailed definitions are provided in the following chapters that are dedicated to each key.

PROFESSIONALISM

Professionalism is the use and display of a set of skills specific to educators. They are attentive of and responsive to administrative and government mandates, they smoothly interact with individuals from various demographics, and they are enthusiastic about teaching and supportive of learning. The four subcategories under professionalism are conduct, knowledge of mandates, interpersonal skills, and attitude.

Conduct applies to a teacher's career path, participation in the educational community, treatment of students, interactions with peers and administrative staff, and efforts with parents.

Knowledge of mandates encompasses the rules that apply to the curriculum, serving special needs students, requirements passed down by federal and state governments, and how governmental requirements impact educational activities.

Interpersonal skills include elements that enhance relationships, such as verbal and nonverbal communication, active listening, social awareness, and self-management.

Attitude encompasses enthusiasm and affection, a sincere concern for students, an appropriate response to negative behaviors, and an interest in outside elements that might impact academic achievement.

PLANNING AND PREPARATION

Planning and preparation are defined as awareness of the activities, curricular goals, materials, and time required to meet the goals of the academic year, each marking period, and weekly and daily units. The four primary elements are knowledge of subject matter, lesson plans, organizational skills, and ongoing staff development.

Knowledge of subject matter involves understanding the curriculum well enough to prepare and present lessons, using content knowledge effectively in the classroom, and the ability to respond to individual learner needs.

Lesson plans encompass individual components such as introduction, instruction, practice, summary, and testing.

Organizational skills revolve around time management, tailoring lessons to the students, and familiarity with the environment.

Ongoing staff development keeps teachers up to date on educational research and trends, emerging classroom technologies, resources, and peer support.

CLASSROOM MANAGEMENT

Classroom management creates an environment in which learning can take place by creating routines, managing disruptions, and building relationships. Classroom management begins with a commonsense approach. To make this process easier, a teacher should display courage, a sense of fairness, and self-confidence. The important elements are supervision, communication, behavior, and environment.

Supervision monitors behaviors, tracks achievements, recognizes areas where students need assistance, provides efficient transitions, and anticipates and eliminates problems.

Communication prompts students with questions, provides time for their responses, and allows the class to respond to major curricular points. The skill utilizes verbal communication, body language, enthusiasm, and an attitude that broadcasts an expectation of success.

Behavior manages negative behaviors, encourages a positive classroom atmosphere, builds strong academic habits, supports individual growth, and develops social skills. Regular and productive outreach to parents is part of this subcategory.

Environment includes the classroom's physical layout, changes to accommodate special lessons, an atmosphere that is safe and welcoming, and a tone focused on academic advancement.

TEACHING WITH RIGOR

Teaching with rigor challenges students to think critically and in a more sophisticated way. Rigor triggers curiosity and expansive intellectual exploration. It moves beyond the textbook and enters real life. The primary elements are instruction, student performance feedback, engagement, and reflective teaching.

Instruction that is rigorous allows students to reflect, requires precision and skill, encourages problem solving, and anticipates exceptional academic achievement.

Student performance feedback enhances personal growth through encouragement, pinpoints weaknesses and provides guidance, and allows freedom in how students approach assignments.

Engagement allows students to demonstrate learning, sparks passion, and links lessons to other subjects and to the real world.

Reflective teaching includes self-observation, self-evaluation, peer observations or research into alternative methods, and student feedback.

TEAMSMANSHIP/SPIRIT OF COOPERATION

Teamsmanship, or the spirit of cooperation, focuses on serving students, parents, and peers. The teachers' networks expand, and the expertise on which they can call grows. Respect for the administration and its needs helps the school reach its goals. And in the classroom, the spirit of cooperation honors cultural diversity. For teamsmanship, the four critical elements are rapport with students, rapport with parents, respect for the administration, and respect for cultural diversity.

Rapport with students builds connections, engages in genuine dialog, encourages a positive outlook, and is delivered with authenticity.

Rapport with parents connects with parents, keeps parents updated, calls on parents to address issues, discovers how to help parents become involved, and discusses the needs of parents.

Respect for the administration builds and maintains relationships with administrators, staff, and peers; expresses gratitude for support; encourages others to grow; and adapts to others.

Respect for cultural diversity recognizes how a student's background shapes his perspective, conveys an open mindset, utilizes diverse teaching methods, and deals sensitively with conflict.

ADMINISTRATIVE DUTIES

The administrative duties teachers perform help the school run smoothly. Everything from attendance and grading papers to managing paraprofessionals supports record keeping and data gathering. Administrative duties also ensure that the curriculum aligns with state and federal mandates. These duties break down into record keeping; paraprofessional management; grading system; and adherence to state, district, and school rules and regulations.

Record keeping involves grades, attendance, notes, and other reports associated with individual students; historical records for lesson plans; and the calendar for the academic year.

Paraprofessional management includes direct supervision of instruction, providing lesson plans, developing a written job description, and creating an environment that supports paraprofessional success.

Grading system duties include recording grades for specific assignments, tracking due dates, implementing different scales for different assignments, and selecting precise and fair methods for grading.

Adherence to state, district, and school rules and regulations covers safety guidelines, state academic statutes, federal education mandates, and school rules.

INSTRUCTION

A teacher's instructional methods and approach must achieve learning results within dynamic classroom, school, and community environments. Since success can be negatively impacted by the increasing pressures on the educational system, adapting instruction to meet those elements is a constant requirement. The four elements for this duty are assessment, technology, cocurricular activities, and differentiated instruction.

Assessment determines student learning achievements, assessing with evidence-based systems and utilizing that knowledge to improve performance results.

Technology includes the proper use of available equipment to enhance learning, engage and empower students, and allow for alternative teaching and learning methods.

Cocurricular activities complement academic goals, enhance personal development, and allow for personal expression.

Differentiated instruction provides a variety of learning avenues to serve preferences and skill levels, develops lesson plans that serve all students, and varies the methods through which students work.

PASTORAL DUTIES

Pastoral elements nurture personal aspects, develop strong relationships, open pathways for personal fulfillment, and nurture physical and psychological well-being. The result is a positive attitude, increased resiliency, better decision-making and risk-assessment skills, and enhanced confidence. The four areas are academic issues; encouragement; communication with peers, administration, and parents; and extracurricular participation.

Academic issues address learning challenges, physical disabilities or illnesses, family situations, and similar events that can negatively impact achievement.

Encouragement involves listening, providing referrals to support services, and acting as a role model.

Communication with peers, administration, and parents develops and maintains connections and ensures that each group or individual is provided information in a timely manner.

Extracurricular participation encourages and supports activities that develop emotional, psychological, and physical well-being.

CORE BEHAVIORAL COMPETENCIES

Behavioral competencies are associated with how teachers approach their roles. Their choices and aptitudes have a profound impact on students, peers, the school, and the community, so a thoughtful approach must relate to all these areas. The four categories involved with this duty are creativity, adaptability, and flexibility; decision-making skills; problem solving; and resilience and tenacity.

Creativity, adaptability, and flexibility include changing course with and without notice, openly receiving feedback, and meeting challenges with solutions.

Decision-making skills utilize information from a variety of sources, apply a broad and multifaceted perspective to consider outcomes and consequences, make a decision, and implement the necessary steps.

Problem solving involves a proactive approach to identifying issues, seeking solutions, considering alternatives, implementing a solution, and evaluating the results.

Resilience and tenacity build self-efficacy, support unwavering dedication, and allow teachers to continue in the face of challenges and to recover quickly after setbacks.

TEACHER AS LEADER

Teachers function as leaders by guiding students through academic challenges as instructional specialists, curriculum experts, and resource providers. They facilitate learning, mentor young minds, and mold personalities. Teachers can also become peer leaders by modeling best practices and professional attitudes. The four areas associated with teacher leadership are modeling lifelong learning, collaborative teaching and learning, system support, and mentoring.

Modeling lifelong learning guides students toward learning resources, pursues additional adult education or career development opportunities, and encourages new approaches to learning.

Collaborative teaching and learning works with small- and large-group activities, implements peer-to-peer learning and feedback, and involves co-teachers.

System support includes helping to solve school-wide issues, participating in an inclusive school culture, and being involved in a collaborative infrastructure.

Mentoring empowers and supports new teachers and individuals who require temporary support and shares best practices.

MOVING FORWARD

Each of the remaining chapters in this section addresses one key responsibility and its associated components. For each of the four components, comments based on real appraisals and classroom situations are provided at each performance tier. Move forward in *The Art of Appraisal* to move your appraisal process up to the top performance tier.

Chapter Four

Professionalism

Professionals in any field have acquired, and continue to acquire, skills specific to their industry. People who act as professionals display an ability that cannot be achieved by others who lack training or experience. Knowledgeable individuals are therefore more effective than anyone else at a particular job. As they gather years of tenure, they are held in higher and higher esteem.

In the field of education, schools must have professional teachers. Those teachers must also display their professionalism while performing their duties and tasks. They must respond to administrative and government mandates and be able to interact with individuals from various demographics associated with age, ethnicity, and socioeconomic status. Their approach must demonstrate enthusiasm and convey their supportive role.

These requirements quite naturally lead us to the four subcategories under professionalism. They are:

- Conduct
- Knowledge of mandates
- Interpersonal skills
- Attitude

Conduct applies to how teachers progress along their career path, their participation in the broader educational community, how they treat students inside their classrooms, their interactions with peers and administrative staff, and their efforts with parents.

Knowledge of mandates encompasses the rules that apply to the curriculum, how special needs can be served, requirements passed down by federal and state governments, and how governmental requirements impact classroom activities.

Interpersonal skills include elements that enhance relationships, such as verbal and nonverbal communication, active listening, social awareness, and the ability to self-manage.

Attitude encompasses the willingness to share personal feelings, such as enthusiasm and affection and warmth that arises from a sincere concern for students; a measured and appropriate response to negative behaviors; and an interest in elements students encounter outside of school that might impact academic achievement.

Teachers who display professionalism put their students first in the classroom. When interacting with peers, they place their concerns at the top of the list and reach out to help whenever possible. With parents, professionalism is displayed by listening deeply and communicating well. Truly professional teachers respect and follow the school's rules and are willing to propose changes that can move the school or district closer to its goals.

Appraisals can correct minor actions that have a big impact, such as encouraging respect for students at every level of ability. They can weave a tighter community by providing feedback on interactions teachers have with peers, staff, and parents. Individuals who appear reluctant to recommend changes can be encouraged to speak their minds. And a community's perspective on the school can be modified by recommending adjustments for how teachers present themselves.

The reason that appraisals can be so powerful in these areas is you. Your training and experience automatically give you the ability to lead teachers to different methods. Because instructors necessarily stay in the classroom for most of the day, they need your perspective on how their activities impact others outside of the classroom. And because you deal so often with parents and the wider community, your understanding of events and trends is invaluable.

Let's explore how actual appraisals have addressed the successes and weaknesses of different teachers in real-world classrooms.

CONDUCT

Conduct applies to a teacher's career path; participation in the educational community; interactions with students, peers, and administrative staff; and outreach to parents.

This evaluation for a second-grade science class demonstrated excellence in conduct:

> Great teachers are the ones who care, who push, who settle for nothing less than excellence for their students; they prepare the launching pad for success in higher education and in life. I see you as such a person, created to make a difference in the educational life of every student who crosses your threshold.

> Your family should be very proud of you and the way you present yourself as a teacher.

> You modeled fairness to all, a compassionate attitude, and the joy to be found in academic achievement. The students are privileged to have a teacher who provides instruction in such a vivid fashion. Students feel your belief in their potential to learn and appreciate science.

This teacher clearly went above and beyond. She was vivacious while presenting the curriculum, which reflected her love of the subject matter. Her lesson plan allowed for clear communication, which allowed students to stay with her the entire time. They were eager to share what they had learned by writing in their journals. Surely, these students will carry that enthusiasm into their futures.

This appraisal of a second-grade social studies class revealed strengths in many areas:

> I was impressed to see how well you handled Monday's observation when you thought I was to observe you on Tuesday. Rather than make excuses, you jumped right in and delivered a good lesson, especially given that you had twice as many students as other teachers.

> You created a classroom atmosphere that inspired students to academic success. You encouraged all students in learning that was meaningful and creative and that required total participation. Your homework assignment provided an opportunity for students to clearly demonstrate their understanding and knowledge of a time line.

> As usual, it was a pleasure to visit with you. I got to observe a lesson provided with strong methods that inspired students to learn and generated a powerful academic environment. I'm sure you have made a name for yourself at this school.

This teacher demonstrated satisfactory performance at several duties. Importantly, her ability to provide strong performance in so many areas at once generated the synergy that creates true professional conduct inside and outside the classroom. Her homework assignment, when reviewed by parents, ensured respect for the school's professionalism. And by performing so well inside the classroom, she has built a positive reputation among peers and with the administration.

These comments for a first-grade mathematics appraisal pinpointed a temporary strength that, given time, could become a weakness:

> I was extremely impressed with the care you gave to preparing for the math lesson. To ensure that you had everything just right, you gave up your lunchtime. By doing this, you exhibited the behavior of a masterful teacher. Howev-

er, try not to give up your lunchtime on a regular basis. It is not the healthiest thing to do.

While every teacher (and principal, of course) will have to occasionally give up personal or free time to ensure that everything operates smoothly, no one should make a habit of this. Everyone needs downtime to relax. By refreshing their minds, teachers return to the classroom with more energy. They are better able to display the leadership and enthusiasm that supports academic success. In this case, a warning from someone who had more experience called out a step that, while it can be effective in the short term, can quickly become detrimental as a habit.

This review for a first-grade language arts block was less than acceptable:

> The Daily Fix-It exercise was not introduced. The chart work was too small for all students to see. One student who raised his hand repeatedly and for prolonged periods was ignored. The teacher walked around the room but did not offer the assistance needed. Instead of providing closure, the teacher stated, "You know you'll get to finish this later."

Some of the flaws in this teacher's performance appear to be unrelated to conduct (the lack of introduction for a task and charts that made learning difficult). However, when combined with the behaviors that clearly are related to conduct, these other flaws point to a lack of enthusiasm for the lesson plans.

These weaknesses also indicate a lack of caring about student achievement because the teacher didn't bother to meet the students' needs. Finally, when the session was closed with a comment that brushed off student distress about not having finished the work, the opportunity to support engagement and a lifelong love of learning was not only lost; it was squashed.

Clearly this teacher's performance in terms of conduct was unacceptable.

KNOWLEDGE OF MANDATES

Knowledge of mandates deals with curricular rules, accommodating special needs, federal and state regulations, and the impact of official mandates.

This visit to a fourth-grade math class yielded exceptional results:

> Your math lesson clearly met the stated instructional objective. The materials you selected fit the subject exceptionally well and ensured that the information was clear. Your use of the overhead projector modeled for students as you delivered the lesson. I observed good, sound, professional practices at work during a child-centered lesson.

The comments for this teacher are noteworthy because the instructor had previously been trained as an accountant. Not only was she able to bring her very high level of education into the classroom; she generated plans and activities that were conveyed in age-appropriate ways. She was able to meet and even exceed the mandates because she had such a deep and broad understanding not only of accounting but also of what students needed to hear.

An appraisal for a third-grade language arts session garnered these comments:

> You developed a unit plan congruent with Georgia state standards. Sufficient time was allowed for students to practice the acquired skill. You posed thought-provoking questions that were specific to the main idea and details. Your students benefit from the way you plan your lessons.

Overall, this teacher met the state mandates with a lesson plan that was well prepared. The unit was broken down into segments that provided enough time for students to practice what they had learned, and their achievement was supported with questions that encouraged participation. Her performance was ranked as Satisfactory.

This review of a third-grade mathematics unit revealed some weaknesses in the teacher's knowledge of mandates:

> Great start! You started with a well-developed plan, and your students came across as eager to learn. However, you must adjust your teaching as needed whenever you check in with students to gauge their level of understanding. Strive to attentively assist students on an individual basis to ensure that their needs are met. Also, provide sufficient time for students to write the required standard.

Although this instructor had performed many of her out-of-class tasks well, she didn't provide enough time for students to perform work that would meet mandates. Her failure to adjust course when it became clear that some students were being left behind didn't support academic achievement for the entire class.

Although she did help students individually, she did not provide the level of focus those students needed. This presents a particularly difficult issue when it comes to meeting educational mandates for the general population and the special needs of certain students. Overall, then, this teacher's performance was ranked as Needs Improvement.

This visit to a fifth-grade reading segment didn't meet mandates:

> You may want to proof your lesson plan; there were quite a few grammatical errors in it. Plans should always be available, even when you are not expecting a supervisory visit. Several actions that could have added quality to the lesson and enhanced learner achievement were not done. The visual aids were un-

clear, and the opening segment did not expose students to the lesson's objectives. This failed to achieve buy-in from the students, and didn't achieve any anticipation of academic success.

Although several elements of this teacher's performance were satisfactory, too many issues revolved around the successful achievement of mandates. In this area, then, the rating was Unsatisfactory.

INTERPERSONAL SKILLS

Interpersonal skills include elements that enhance relationships, such as verbal and nonverbal communication, active listening, social awareness, and the ability to self-manage.

This sixth-grade social studies class was found to be particularly lucky:

> The plan reflected a child-centered approach to imparting knowledge. You maintained a professional demeanor throughout the lesson. Your enthusiasm and energetic delivery were notable. Sharing your personal journey from Liberia to America was quite fitting for this lesson. Students seemed intrigued and inquisitive about every detail.

The ability of this teacher to engage her students in the lesson and in real-world anecdotes that applied directly to that lesson resulted in exceptional performance. In addition to the strong lesson plan and her communication skills, this instructor engaged students by sharing personal information. Because she connected so directly with the students, the education they received was deep and sure to be long-lasting.

A third-grade science class benefited from the teacher's sound skills:

> She exhibited fairness and patience toward students, and she offered lots of praise and encouragement. I observed respect for cultural diversity. She used a modulated tone of voice to lend excitement to the lesson. However, I did not hear the lesson closure. Closure is that important time when the teacher wraps up a lesson plan and helps students organize the information into a meaningful context in their minds.

Even though the lesson covered a topic that usually excites students, the teacher didn't make full use of their engagement. Most of her interpersonal skills were sound, and considering the age of the classroom, she demonstrated an appropriate level of patience.

But since the ending portion of the lesson was missing, she failed to cement what had been learned in a way that ensured both comprehension and long-term recall. Overlooking this important element can be viewed as a failure to understand how her students can achieve results that take them to a new level. This teacher therefore received a rating of Satisfactory.

This third-grade math class had some issues that needed to be addressed:

> Your delivery for the most part lacked strong confidence. It could have been because there were quite a few outside interruptions on that morning. I have every confidence that you are going to be fine once you get over your nervousness and build your confidence. Remember that you have people cheering you on in the direction of success, and we won't let you fail!

In this case, the core issue related to self-management. The teacher lacked confidence in her ability to control classroom behaviors, which meant each outside interruption took longer to get under control. She also was more frazzled by the interruptions than she should have been, pointing to an inability to control her emotional response to unexpected intrusions. Her communication and interpersonal connections suffered. The rank given was Needs Improvement . . . along with encouraging words to help bolster her self-esteem.

Over the course of several visits to a sixth-grade math class, the evaluator observed persistent errors in one teacher's efforts:

> Place your decimals at the baseline. Double-check your math answers before providing them to the students. Remember to offer more words of encouragement for correct answers. Circulate throughout the classroom to ensure participation, and review strategies to use with uncooperative students.

At this grade level, disruptive students can destroy a classroom environment with their outbursts and by undermining the teacher's authority. When joined with the other interpersonal failures, such as a lack of praise and allowing some students to zone out during class, this teacher was having a really hard time.

Adding to the issue was the instructor's constant mistakes. A few errors are going to happen to anyone, but this individual was making some pretty basic errors. And those errors were repeated even after having been pointed out. This lack of understanding around the curriculum further erodes any respect students might otherwise offer and makes it even more difficult to connect with them. This teacher's performance was therefore rated Unacceptable.

ATTITUDE

Attitude encompasses the willingness to share personal feelings, such as enthusiasm and affection and warmth that arises from a sincere concern for students; a measured and appropriate response to negative behaviors; and an interest in elements that students encounter outside of school that might impact academic achievement.

This review of a kindergarten language arts class recorded stellar performance:

> The lesson plan offered a fun, high-energy program that kept students engaged. You owned the lesson and the room from beginning to end. It was evident that you have achieved a mastery in the classroom. You displayed energy and enthusiasm for teaching, and you came across as someone who will work tirelessly to see to it that all students who enter through your classroom door will be effectively taught. Kudos!

This woman's attitude had a great deal to do with her sterling performance. The lesson plans she put together proved that she was as enthusiastic about teaching outside the classroom as when she stepped into the school. Her students were engaged, and she gave plenty of praise when it was deserved. These students were clearly being set up for success, so the rating was Excellent.

An appraisal of a third-grade social studies class found a satisfactory level of performance:

> Planned activities in ways that made learning fun. Corrected inappropriate behaviors without disturbing the learning process. Throughout, you demonstrated a professional and positive attitude along with patience.

The teacher cared enough to find ways to make the lessons engaging and exciting for this age level. She also utilized a personal and very warm method of addressing negative behaviors that allowed the rest of the class to continue working while the student who acted out was brought back into line. All of this was supported by the patience and professionalism expected of a teacher, so her performance was rated as Satisfactory.

An observation of a kindergarten math unit discovered behavioral issues linked to the teacher's attitude:

> Your comments to me at the end of the lesson were on point. We tend to want students to like us, so we try to become friends with them. That never seems to work in the classroom, so always strive for students to respect you as you consistently reinforce standards of classroom behavior.

In this case, the teacher was working too hard to get the kids to like her. She needed instead to ensure that they respected her and her authority. Anyone who has been in charge of a classroom knows that a little attitude adjustment goes a long way. During a short debriefing after the session, the teacher recognized where her problems lay and was ready to adjust course. The assessment resulted in a rating of Needs Improvement.

An eighth-grade literature unit revealed deeper issues in things that might tend to slip by unnoticed:

> Please show respect for all learners regardless of their current level of skill. Use an appropriate tone of voice when addressing students, and show more enthusiasm for the job of teaching.

Although comments on other performance areas detailed satisfactory achievements, the teacher's attitude was less than stellar. A flat, almost bored demeanor did nothing to encourage excitement for learning or engagement. When the educational leader can't be bothered to care about teaching, how can we expect students to care about learning? This performance was rated as Unacceptable.

CONCLUSION

Professional teachers understand the mandates to meet and implement lesson plans accordingly. Their interpersonal skills allow them to work with students and teachers, parents, and administrators. Their conduct is always above reproach, and their attitudes create an engaging and exciting educational environment.

Appraisals that offer feedback on specifics that might otherwise go unnoticed, that offer minor course corrections, and that point out and commend strengths enhance the benefits students receive. A supervisor's advanced training and experience can support good habits and provide different options for weaker ones. Work with the four elements of professionalism to supercharge your school on its way to the top.

Chapter Five

Planning and Preparation

Before a teacher steps into the classroom every day, quite a bit of planning and preparation must already have been accomplished. Annual overviews have to be prepared before the start of the academic year to ensure that educational goals are met. Each marking period has its own trajectory that is further broken down into weekly and daily units.

For each of these segments, a teacher must know which activities will take place, how each activity relates to curricular goals, and how lessons will link to other subjects. The appropriate materials must be gathered or created; time must be allotted in appropriate measures; and noncurricular needs, such as fundraisers, schoolwide activities, and safety drills, must be accommodated.

To start out well and stay the course, the four primary elements of planning and preparation are:

- Knowledge of subject matter
- Lesson plans
- Organizational skills
- Ongoing staff development

Knowledge of subject matter involves having a deep enough understanding of the curriculum to effectively prepare and present lessons, using content knowledge effectively in the classroom, recognizing when individual students are struggling, and being equipped to respond to individual learner needs.

Lesson plans break down into the individual components of a plan, which includes introduction, instruction, practice, summary, and testing. This does not involve the format in which the plans are prepared or presented unless the format itself creates issues.

Organizational skills revolve around time management, tailoring lessons to the current group of students, and familiarity with the working environment.

Ongoing staff development keeps teachers up to date on educational research and trends, emerging classroom technologies, changes in resources, and the efforts of peers.

Planning and preparation is truly a year-round activity. Dedicated teachers will continue learning and growing even when school is out. They bring new ideas and fresh perspectives into the classroom by implementing different plans, adjusting time management skills, and implementing small changes that reap big results.

Because planning and preparation require so much time and effort, the appraisal process can offer significant help. Comments that address small matters can control elements that, since they are present during all activities, need to be managed well. Teachers who implement new ideas need an outsider's perspective to verify that things are working as intended.

In addition to these types of notes, an appraisal can pull in the wisdom of peers. Individual instructors probably can't connect with every other teacher in their school, but the principal knows what's going on in each classroom. Through written appraisals and follow-up feedback sessions, techniques used in other departments or classrooms can benefit every teacher.

KNOWLEDGE OF SUBJECT MATTER

Knowledge of subject matter draws on a broad understanding of the subject, uses that knowledge to enhance academic achievement, recognizes students who are struggling, and responds to individual learner needs.

This appraisal of a second-grade math class revealed an exceptional level of understanding:

> You showed great interest in your students' ability to master the lesson objective. I saw you enthusiastically reaching out to individual students to make sure they understood. I imagine that you spend countless hours away from school searching for ways and ideas to enrich your lesson plans and lesson deliveries. They are signs of a teacher who is passionate about teaching and learning.

This instructor clearly went above and beyond. She demonstrated a knowledge of the subject that allowed her to build lesson plans and ensure academic excellence. When individual students faltered, she presented the same knowledge in ways those individuals could grasp. Not only was this teacher inspired to pass on knowledge; she clearly continued learning on her own.

This visit to a second-grade science classroom focused on a unit about force and motion:

> Your content knowledge was appropriate for the lesson. You checked for understanding using open-ended questions. Your instructional strategies were relevant to achieving the objective. You built the lesson on prior knowledge about force and motion. You communicated and presented material clearly and checked for understanding.

This teacher turned in a satisfactory performance. Her understanding of the curriculum's content was appropriate for the knowledge she needed to convey. It was also broad enough to assist with comprehension. Importantly, she tied the lessons to prior units on the same topic, placing students on a foundation from which to advance.

A visit to a third-grade language arts class revealed a few places for improvement:

> Although meaningful, the lesson was brief. The lesson could have been enhanced by linking the day's activities to lessons learned on previous days. This also would have eliminated the time management issue of scrambling to fill the remaining time with a different activity.

Generally, this teacher did well, though she displayed a little difficulty connecting her understanding of the topic to the level of her students. She underestimated their ability to grasp the lesson's meaningful concepts. She ended up with extra time that needed to be filled productively. Whenever a teacher has to pull forward elements of the next day's lesson, students lose valuable time. This element was therefore rated as Needs Improvement. Specific comments adjusted her approach so that she would be better prepared.

This first-grade language arts appraisal revealed a critical flaw:

> The lesson plan did not contain enough components to adequately address the curriculum mandates. Give attention to the lesson opening, one that states what is about to happen and why. Check in with students periodically to recognize those who are struggling. Give attention to providing a lesson closure.

> In summary, I thought you came across as caring and concerned about the lesson you were delivering. The main concern is always, are students learning? To achieve that, remember to always plan your work and work your plan.

In this case, there was a failure to communicate the level of information required. Although the instructor clearly cared, failure resulted from an insufficiently broad understanding of the topic. The lack of an opening and closing did not prepare students to learn nor did it cement in their minds what they had learned. Teachers must be able to present information in multiple ways. This ensures that the lead-in to a lesson anticipates success and that the closure of the lesson builds a long-term foundation for continuous progress. The instructor's performance was rated as Unsatisfactory.

LESSON PLANS

Lesson plan elements focus on the individual components of a lesson plan, such as introduction, instruction, practice, summary, and testing.

An appraisal for a fifth-grade social studies unit addressed the Great Depression:

> The opening activity established a solid foundation for new information and supported the lesson's goals. You constructed the lesson in a manner that made the content relevant to the interests of fifth-graders.
>
> You posed questions and conducted the discussion specific to the skill/content being taught. You taught to the objectives and made maximum use of instructional resources, materials, and time. The closure clearly reviewed the lesson objectives and learning tasks. Great job all around!

This instructor performed exceptionally well. The instruction met curriculum standards. To ensure enthusiasm, content was tied to the interests of this particular age group. The lesson was bracketed by an opening and a closing that supported the lesson's goals. All this was possible only with the correct layout of a lesson plan that went beyond the textbook. The rating was Excellent.

A visit to a fifth-grade science class determined that the lesson plan met expectations:

> During the opening, you communicated the scope and sequence of the content to be covered. You engaged students in hands-on activities to aid in their understanding and mastery of the circuit. You utilized a variety of questioning techniques to ascertain learning. Your students reap dividends from your investment of time in creating quality lesson plans.

The teacher began the lesson with an opening that was pointed. This focus on the lesson was maintained throughout. The hands-on techniques engaged students and allowed individuals and groups to practice what they had learned. This instructor's lesson plan was ranked as Satisfactory.

For a second-grade grammar class, the observation noted two areas for improvement:

> You started the lesson by gaining students' attention and by linking the lesson to yesterday's lesson. You honored the timeframe for the lesson plan. You asked key questions about the story read aloud to keep students focused and continuously paying attention. The lesson appealed to students and was appropriate for the curriculum and aligned to the goals of the lesson.
>
> In the future, be sure to open with a statement about the lesson itself. Also, note that a good lesson should come to an end with a closure of some kind. It helps tie all of the learning together and makes that lasting impression. Please make sure your lessons have an appropriate opening and closing.

The primary components of the lesson plan worked well. The content was age appropriate and of interest to young minds. The methods used to maintain attention and keep the students moving forward were effective and deployed with skill. But even a strong lesson such as this one can fail if the opening and closing segments aren't presented in ways that strengthen learning.

In this case, an opening was offered to tie the unit to prior knowledge. However, the lesson itself was launched without any preamble. Students weren't prepared to focus on the new content, which might hamper comprehension. For the opening and the closing, then, the rating of the lesson plan was Needs Improvement.

An appraisal for a kindergarten language arts class revealed significant problems:

> The activities planned for this guided reading session were appropriate to the age level. They were not congruent with the stated objectives of the lesson plan. Because of this, they did not meet the standards mandated by the state.
>
> You posed questions that required students to think about the story. You provided verbal feedback and praise. Your learning materials were not handy or ready for use when they were needed. Due to the time lost managing these errors, insufficient time was left in class for lesson closure.

In this case, the teacher engaged enthusiastically with students and provided materials that met their interests and captured their attention. Unfortunately, the effort to connect with them and maintain their focus sent the lesson plan off its target. Mandates weren't met, and students were not guided toward the lesson. This performance was rated as Unsatisfactory.

ORGANIZATIONAL SKILLS

Organizational skills revolve around time management, tailoring lessons to the current group of students, and familiarity with the environment.

A third-grade language arts unit on cause and effect benefited from exceptional organizational skills:

> Plans showed evidence of preparation of a variety of interactive tasks that richly complemented the content being covered. Activities were planned that related to students' knowledge base, interests, and life experiences. Throughout the lesson, students were encouraged to think and problem solve.
>
> Your creative use of real-life examples gave students an excellent insight into the main concept. By increasing comprehension and engagement, you utilized every minute of available class time. Transitions between tasks were smooth and well thought out.

This instructor had organizational skills in aces. By utilizing the interests and experiences of her students, she ensured that they remained focused. She was therefore able to further engage them by asking questions and providing real-world examples. All this rich and deep instruction was enabled by superior organizational skills. Her performance was ranked as Excellent.

A third-grade math unit was found to be well organized:

> Gave timely and helpful feedback to students. Monitored students' progress throughout the lesson. Planned and implemented a child-centered activity. Kept plan congruent with the stated objectives. Posed questions that were specific to the skills being taught.

This instructor utilized activities and questions to keep students focused and moving forward. By monitoring their progress, she ensured that the class would meet curricular standards. She achieved a rating of Satisfactory.

The appraisal of a third-grade science lab on holding in heat revealed a strong teacher with one significant weakness:

> Instructional method was geared toward stimulating interest in the subject matter. The plan clearly focused on the student's perspective and reached them where they stand. Strategies geared toward engaging all students in the lesson activities were outlined. Materials reflected a belief in the credo that "children learn best by doing."
>
> In the future, model sample experiments to illustrate expected outcomes. Students will then gain a better understanding of what to do and what is expected of them from beginning to end.

It's critical that students understand what is expected of them. Nothing outlines the steps better than acting out the experiment. The teacher should have used the equipment to demonstrate, step by step, what was required to cut down on the need for assistance. Learning results would have been enhanced, and academic achievement would have been met at a much higher level. This observation resulted in a rating of Needs Improvement.

An appraisal for a first-grade math class pinpointed several failures:

> You used name sticks to call on some students; however, names created a problem from time to time. Next time, practice ahead of time with pronunciation. This will avoid some of the disruption that occurred in the classroom.

> The lesson engaged whole- and small-group activities. You modeled the activities for the small groups, but the lesson plan itself was overly ambitious. Having four groups rotate through all the tasks was far too much. Insufficient time was allowed for each task to be completed by the group, leading to students being unable to practice what they had been taught.

> Materials provided were written too small for some students to read easily. Additionally, the notes made on the board were too small for most students to view. A focus on best practices was not in evidence.

This plan and its implementation were rife with organizational failures. Perhaps the most critical was the inability of the teacher to recognize age-appropriate materials and activities. The lesson plan was too ambitious in terms of activities. In addition to falling short of student academic goals, this teacher also made comprehension difficult.

Her continuous difficulty pronouncing names disrupted the class and likely alienated individual students. Her failure to plan appropriately and organize well resulted in a less than optimal educational experience. This would not encourage enthusiasm or engagement in her classroom. This performance was rated as Unsatisfactory.

ONGOING STAFF DEVELOPMENT

Ongoing staff development provides information on current research and trends, new and revamped classroom technologies, changes in available resources, and ways to garner support from peers.

One observation of a seventh-grade math class revealed a teacher who works hard to keep up with developmental elements:

> I observed that you encourage students to actively participate during the delivery of instruction. You utilized smart board technology as an effective teaching method. As you conducted the lesson walk-through, you provided clear directions, relevant examples, and excellent feedback. You challenged your students to consider the lesson deeply and to resolve issues relating to the curriculum.

This instructor was clearly putting in the time needed to keep her skills relevant. She utilized the smart board to provide information as well as to engage students in active participation. Additionally, she connected with students by relating the work tasks to relevant and timely events important to their lives. This teacher clearly was involved in a lot of ongoing developmental opportunities and connected with her peers. She achieved a rating of Excellent.

A sixth-grade math class also enjoyed a strong performance by the teacher:

> You taught to the objective and used effective teaching practices. The use of stickers and the timer kept students focused and motivated to solve the problems. You planned creative and productive group activities to utilize the class period and enhanced the learning experience. For some students, math is not an easy subject to master. You made learning fun. Do continue to seek creative ways to challenge your students!

This instructor performed well by utilizing methods that turned math into a game. She also pulled in materials that were tactile (the stickers). This unique approach came from being exposed to the methods used by her peers. Her performance, based on her outreach to teachers of other subjects, allowed her to achieve a rating of Satisfactory.

A visit to a kindergarten math class revealed one area where the teacher could improve through peer support or additional development:

> The rules of the game used to demonstrate and allow practice of the math concepts had to be continuously explained and reinforced. Do be more mindful of kindergarteners' attention spans. While the content was well matched with their efforts, the complexity of the game turned out to be a bit confusing. Consider providing more variety in the learning activities and experiences to allow students to think beyond the game itself.

In this situation, the teacher had several options for how she could have provided a stronger experience. She might have asked a peer to review the rules of the game to ensure that they weren't too complex. She might have selected a different game from online resources that offer free materials. Because she did not, the classroom suffered. Her performance was therefore rated as Needs Improvement.

An appraisal of a fourth-grade math unit uncovered poor results:

> The lesson did not have the depth and breadth that it should have had to meet lesson objectives. It would have been helpful if you had created a cheat sheet for students to use as a quick-reference tool for fraction facts. The planned activities were not appropriate for the state's curriculum objectives.

This teacher needed to refresh her understanding of her state's goals and objectives. The unit fell short of the level of understanding students needed. If the instructor's performance was allowed to continue at that level, her class would not gain enough knowledge to succeed at the next grade level. Her rating was therefore Unsatisfactory.

CONCLUSION

Planning and preparation is a multipronged duty to which teachers must constantly apply effort. From the overarching plan for the academic year right down to the daily units, a teacher must set up activities that relate to curricular goals and, optimally, ones that interlink lessons learned in other subjects.

Knowledge of the subject, the details of the lesson plans, an individual's organizational skills, and staff development allow the dedicated teacher to learn and grow alongside students. The appraisal process provides new ideas and fresh perspectives from the principal and other staff. When teachers are led to excellence through comments and feedback, students excel at school and at life.

Chapter Six

Classroom Management

Classroom management provides an environment in which learning can take place. For some classes, it can feel like herding cats; in others, students form a cohesive group that works well together and is respectful from day one.

Creating routines that build good habits, managing disruptions in firm yet compassionate ways, and building relationships with and between students are critical. A classroom that is directed with best practices becomes a tiny community that focuses on the common goal of learning.

The key elements associated with effective classroom management are:

- Supervision
- Communication
- Behavior
- Environment

Supervision encompasses monitoring student behaviors, tracking student achievements and areas where they need assistance, implementing effective leadership techniques, efficiently transitioning between tasks, and anticipating problems so they can be eliminated or at least minimized.

Communication involves elements such as prompting students with questions; providing time for students to respond; using words, body language, and attitude to convey an expectation of success; and utilizing enthusiasm to focus attention and inspire engagement.

Behavior is associated with managing negative traits and encouraging positive ones, building strong academic habits, encouraging individual growth, and developing students' social skills. Since activities in the home can impact behavior in school, regular and productive outreach to parents is part of this subcategory.

Environment includes the physical layout of the classroom for everyday activities and how it changes to accommodate special lessons and an atmosphere that is welcoming and academically supportive.

Classroom management is a commonsense approach to existing issues and potential problems combined with hands-on action. The skills needed to integrate these actions become better with practice; during practice, the commonsense approach also matures. A sense of fairness is required. It goes without saying that courage and self-confidence are part of the mix!

This is one area of responsibility where an appraisal can make a huge impact, even for experienced teachers. A classroom's atmosphere changes with every new group of students who arrive at the beginning of the year. It also can change day by day depending on what's happening with families, in the school, and in the wider community. Effective classroom management can therefore seem like a moving target and can frustrate even the most tenured educator.

A fresh perspective is always of value. In addition to your own experience in education, you can see student behavior from an outsider's perspective. Because you don't deal with a specific classroom every hour of every day, you can spot the causes of problems and bring new ideas to the management of recognized issues.

SUPERVISION

Supervision involves monitoring behavior in the classroom; tracking academic achievement; effectively leading; efficiently transitioning; and eliminating or minimizing other types of problems.

For a fifth-grade social studies lesson, the teacher received the following comments:

> The lesson followed a logical and interesting sequence, thereby eliminating the need to address behavioral interruptions. You asked many questions to gauge comprehension. You used your time wisely and displayed energy and enthusiasm. I like the fact that you appeared confident and poised while teaching.

These comments reflect an excellent level of performance. Comprehension, which ties into academic achievement, was monitored by asking questions. Efficient transitions were achieved by paving a superior pathway through the lesson's components. Leadership qualities were apparent in the individual's poise and confidence. Issues were eliminated using class time efficiently, with smooth transitions, and by engaging students through their enthusiasm.

This next comment comes from an appraisal for a third-grade reading/language arts unit:

> Because you planned such an interesting and informative lesson, students were attentive and well behaved. You conducted a meaningful class discussion on narratives.

Here, the teacher did well with the lesson plan, content, and curriculum objectives. These elements kept students engaged and attentive, which prevented behavioral issues from cropping up. Meaningful content and a discussion kept the class on task in a way that met mandated goals.

This comment, provided for a sixth-grade mathematics unit, pinpoints one area of weakness:

> Circulate more throughout the classroom to ensure participation.

In this case, only nine students were present. Although the comment is short and targets the only weakness discovered during the observation, the fact that the class was so small proved that the weakness absolutely must be addressed. There really wasn't any reason why every student couldn't have participated actively, so the teacher's failure to engage the entire classroom truly needed attention.

This eighth-grade mathematics observation revealed a deeper issue:

> I do not feel that you exhibited a take-charge attitude during the lesson delivery. This strength is critical to effectively delivering a lesson that you put hours into planning. You show great potential, so I know you will accept these suggestions in the spirit in which they are given.

In this area, the teacher's performance was rated as Unsatisfactory. While it can be difficult for substitutes and co-teachers to gain control of an established classroom during short engagements, leadership, and confidence must be developed from day one. This teacher needed to step up to support academic performance.

COMMUNICATION

Communication involves prompting students to participate, allowing students to share their perspectives, conveying the expectation of success, focusing attention on the task, and inspiring a love of learning.

Here's a commentary provided for a seventh-grade science class:

> You used appropriate facial and physical behaviors, gestures, and language; you exhibited appropriate confidence and poise in working with students. Time was effectively used and managed, and the lesson followed a logical sequence. If I had not known better, I would have thought I was observing a seasoned teacher. I thoroughly enjoyed watching you at work in the classroom.

Students were motivated to learn and fully engaged. The teacher used various communication channels, such as words, facial expressions, and body language, to generate a dynamic delivery. Communication and comprehension were supported by the sequence of the lesson plan. Clearly this teacher deserved a rating of Excellent.

By comparison, this fifth-grade English class illuminates the difference between Excellent and Satisfactory:

> This was an impressive undertaking, to address all forms of figurative language at one time, but you did a phenomenal job! You clearly communicated expectations for learning and opened with a relevant anticipatory set activity that set the tone for lesson success. You stressed the definitions and important points concerning each type of figurative language in a step-by-step process. Students could focus on small pieces at a time before moving on to the next one.
>
> Sharing life experiences related to the subject matter made students pay close attention and kept them interested and on task. You utilized a variety of questioning techniques along with using instructional time wisely. Opportunities were provided for students to apply newly acquired knowledge.
>
> You placed value on the contribution of each student and challenged them to think critically. You provided clarification and praise when needed.

In this case, the teacher did everything expected. He clearly laid out learning expectations and conveyed his anticipation of academic success. The step-by-step approach allowed students to fully grasp each element. Techniques to keep their attention were utilized, and all individuals were encouraged to participate. The performance was marked as Satisfactory.

This commentary for a first-grade math unit relates strengths with an associated weakness:

> During the lesson, students were required to speak, read, and write information related to the lesson. You challenged students to perform by engaging them in activities that served to support and assist with lesson mastery.
>
> Remember to sprinkle more praise throughout your lesson.

In this classroom, the teacher ensured that every student participated in active learning. Students were challenged and rose to the challenge; however, the teacher's response was not as encouraging as it could have been. At every age, children need to hear that they are doing well. This is particularly important with a class this young, so this performance was ranked as Needs Improvement.

Another first-grade observation, this one in language arts, had several small issues that added up to a big problem:

> Give attention to a lesson opening, one that states what is about to happen and why. Scan the room periodically for raised hands. The Daily Fix It print size appeared to be too small for all students to adequately see. Give attention to providing a lesson closure. As you monitor seat work, offer encouragement to students.

In this case, the teacher failed to support the curriculum by providing overviews before and after the lesson. Students who wanted to participate did not receive that opportunity. The materials were difficult to utilize, which forced students to decipher the materials before they could focus on the content. The lack of encouragement, particularly with students who were eager to engage, was especially disappointing. Overall, this teacher's performance was Unsatisfactory.

BEHAVIOR

Behavior includes managing negative traits and encouraging positive ones, builds strong academic habits, encourages individual growth, and builds social skills. Since lessons and activities in the home can have an impact in school, regular and productive outreach to parents is part of this subcategory.

Here is a set of comments for an eight-grade mathematics class:

> You encouraged students by continuously modeling expectations. Ongoing feedback was offered to maintain focused participation in the lesson. You made maximum use of instructional time, and you demonstrated the ability to motivate students. Positive instructional strategies were employed to promote learning. Students were privileged to have you provide math instruction in such an imaginative, innovative, competent, and exciting way!

This individual achieved a rating of Excellent because she supercharged all the goals found at the Satisfactory level. Expectations were modeled throughout the lesson, feedback was offered continuously, and every moment of available time was put to productive use. The creative aspects of the lesson's planning and implementation took this class above and beyond and kept students focused entirely on classroom activities.

This fourth-grade reading lesson remained steadily at the expected level:

> You modeled expected behavior, and you maintained a firm and caring reading group despite one student's constant interruptions. I observed fairness and patience toward all students. You managed time well and you were quite professional throughout the visit.

While providing accurate and honest comments, the appraisal also supported the teacher's efforts to decrease the potentially negative impact of one student's behavior. Additional comments marked the teacher's poise and professionalism. The performance was ranked as Satisfactory.

This portion of an appraisal for an elementary social studies unit was preceded by comments on the teacher's strengths:

> The area that needs some attention is with consistently getting and maintaining students' attentive behaviors throughout your lessons. Today's observation was one of those lessons where students were not as cooperative as they should have been. Perhaps it was because they had just returned from recess.
>
> Consistently enforce the classroom code of conduct. Eliminate choral responses. Require students to raise their hands and wait to be called on before speaking. Require students to remain in their seats during class unless the lesson calls for other activity. Practice assertiveness.

The teacher needed to improve in several areas that impacted student behaviors. A handful of specific, actionable steps that could address the issues quickly and easily were recommended.

An eight-grade mathematics teacher faced more pressing issues:

> It is important to anticipate and avoid student off-task behavior. Work on requiring students to acknowledge and self-correct unproductive behaviors. Know the classroom code of conduct and consistently enforce it.

This teacher failed to anticipate and eliminate off-task behavior. While students might not act out in a truly negative fashion, any type of behavior that doesn't relate to the lesson has the potential to disrupt the entire classroom. The academic performance of the group suffers. This teacher needed to be told to know the code of conduct for his classroom as well as to enforce it, leading to a ranking of Unsatisfactory.

ENVIRONMENT

The *environment* includes a room's standard physical layout, the use of space for special lessons, and an atmosphere that is supportive emotionally and academically.

This brief comment from a kindergarten mathematics unit shows how a single element of performance can lift a teacher in the appraisal process:

> You provided a nurturing and supportive atmosphere for learning. You also demonstrated a high degree of professionalism. From this observation, you show great promise as a master teacher!

Overall, everything this teacher did in class was in line with expectations. What lifted the performance was the effort to provide a warm and welcoming environment. Much of that came from the teacher's professional attitude, a nurturing demeanor, and interactions with students. Truly, this demonstrated a great performance by someone well on her way to total excellence.

This observation is from an Algebra II class with a mixed group of ninth-grade through twelfth-grade students:

> The classroom arrangement was very appropriate for this type of instruction. You provided opportunities for students to engage in independent math practice, and you showed proficient use of white board technology.

The room's layout allowed for group and individual instruction and learning. Available equipment was utilized in ways that enhanced the lesson plan. Since the environment supported learning that met expectations, the rating was Satisfactory.

An elementary social studies class revealed an area where environmental logistics needed improvement:

> Identify a more structured way to collect students' finished work. For example, have students remain seated as you collect their work, or identify a student to collect it for you.

In this case, allowing students to get out of their seats to turn in their work disrupted the environment. A prior observation for the same teacher revealed several environment issues, so this visit was focused entirely on classroom management. The teacher showed significant improvement but still needed to make adjustments in one area. While the entire appraisal received a Satisfactory rating, this one element remained under Needs Improvement.

A third-grade science class had more significant issues:

> Work needs to be done in becoming proficient with classroom technology. Establish the rules of engagement for hands-on lessons.

While much of this teacher's other performance aspects were acceptable, significant issues showed up in the use of classroom technology. This can negatively impact learning in any classroom, but in a science class, it's really a prerequisite for the teacher. The same logic applied to hands-on activities. Since so much of a science lab can involve activities, utilizing the environment to keep students focused and clear rules about each activity are necessary. These comments reflected a rating of Unsatisfactory.

CONCLUSION

Classroom management is one of the key responsibilities a teacher must implement fully and effectively. Building an environment in which learning can take place is accomplished by creating routines, managing disruptions, and building relationships with and between students through supervision, communication, behaviors, and the environment.

A commonsense approach combined with hands-on actions, a sense of fairness, and self-confidence allows teachers to develop this necessary skill. An appraisal that provides specific and actionable feedback, pinpoints weaknesses, praises strengths, and provides a fresh perspective can have a huge impact. Focus on the four primary aspects outlined in this chapter to enable every teacher to excel at classroom management.

Chapter Seven

Teaching with Rigor

Teaching with rigor isn't about heavy student workloads or the difficulty of assignments. Instead, it's about challenging students to do more than memorize answers they think will be on the test. When instructors teach with rigor, they challenge young minds to think critically and in a more sophisticated way.

Importantly, rigor triggers curiosity, a love of lessons that feed that curiosity, and a more expansive way of thinking. It moves beyond the textbook and enters real life. Rigor, then, is all about inspiring passion for every component of the curriculum.

The primary elements of rigor can be categorized as:

- Instruction
- Student performance feedback
- Engagement
- Reflective teaching

Instruction that is rigorous allows time for students to reflect before responding, requires students to work with precision and skill, encourages inventive problem solving, and anticipates exceptional academic achievement . . . no matter where a student's skill level is at the start of the year.

Student performance feedback enhances students' personal growth through encouragement and praise, pinpoints their weaknesses and then provides them guidance on how to address those weaknesses, and supports their efforts by allowing them freedom in how they approach assignments.

Engagement involves the demonstration of learning, sparking passion for the curriculum's content, and linking lessons to other subjects and to the real world. Engagement can include those times when one student is asked to comment on another student's observations, which creates an upward spiral of discussion and communication.

Reflective teaching includes self-observation inside the classroom, self-evaluation outside the classroom, peer observations, or research into alternative methods, and student feedback.

Teaching with rigor creates a classroom environment in which exploration is encouraged, discoveries are made, conclusions are linked to real events, and students' lives are enhanced by a sense of challenge and achievement. Young minds discover that grit and determination reap real results. They become more willing to tackle the curriculum and succeed by their own measures of success.

The appraisal process mirrors teaching with rigor. It encourages educational professionals to step outside their comfort zones and reach for more. Comments and feedback enable them to address areas where they are weak. A new perspective guides them toward solutions. Best of all, the appraisal can supercharge even a top performer's results.

With the wisdom of experience and the broad view of the entire school, a principal can provide small tips or introduce easy techniques that open the door to greater success for every professional. The appraisal process allows for many opportunities to propose a new approach for classrooms. A rigorous appraisal supports teaching with rigor.

INSTRUCTION

Instruction should allow time for reflection, require precision and skill, encourage problem solving, and anticipate academic achievement from all students.

An appraisal of a second-grade social studies unit discovered a teacher utilizing all the components of rigorous instruction:

> You utilized positive reinforcement and encouragement. You created a classroom atmosphere that inspired students to academic success. You gave clear directions and explanations. You taught for cognitive understanding. You encouraged all students in learning that was meaningful and creative and that required total participation.

This teacher posed questions to assess student understanding and to get them thinking about how they would respond. She challenged them with assignments that allowed them to practice the lesson and demonstrate their learning. In every way, her challenges inspired students to achieve more. Her performance was rated as Excellent.

This ninth-grade honors geography class showed rigorous instruction at a different level:

> You communicated expectations and began the lesson with a warm-up activity related to prior learning. You asked probing questions and entertained questions. You provided precise explanations while students took notes and watched videos. Positive reinforcement led to students being engaged and well behaved.

The teacher in this case provided a strong level of rigor in her instructional methods. Since she was leading an honors class, however, the challenges could have been more intense. While she allowed students to ask questions, she could have allowed them to provide their own answers. This additional challenge could have helped each student and the class as a whole reach beyond their already high academic success. Her performance was rated as Satisfactory.

In an evaluation for an elementary social studies class, one of the teacher's habits interfered with how students could respond to rigorous instruction:

> It is hard to point out information on the Promethean board without your body getting in the way of the viewers. So I would suggest the use of a pointer or yardstick when trying to point out and/or clarify information.

At first, this appears to be a slight matter hardly worthy of comment, but when students are appropriately challenged, the flow of information must be seamless. A simple matter like blocking parts of the board becomes an additional challenge. Because this class was exceptionally large, blocking any portion of the board left large sections of the class unable to follow along. It was therefore an area marked Needs Improvement.

A visit to a first-grade language arts class revealed some pressing issues:

> At the beginning of the lesson, write the objectives on the board, and have students repeat those objectives. Ask students to define key components of the lesson plan as you define each of them. Help them provide you with an answer by probing with additional leading questions. When you read from a book, use appropriate strategies to ensure that all students can view the pictures.

This teacher was clearly struggling with engaging her students rigorously. By failing to convey expectations in a way that students could understand and recall, she lost the opportunity to have a thoughtful reading session. The inability of some students to view the illustrations meant that they lost the visual component that would enhance understanding. The failure to allow students time to respond thoughtfully or on their own left the class with a lesson that meant little. Her performance was rated as Unsatisfactory.

STUDENT PERFORMANCE FEEDBACK

Student performance feedback uses encouragement and praise to enhance students' personal growth, calls out and provides guidance for addressing their weaknesses, and allows them to approach assignments in ways that fit their learning preferences.

An observation of a third-grade reading and language arts class had several positive elements:

> You provided hands-on activities and allowed individual students to vary the method of completion. You used appropriate visuals as a foundation for probing questions. You monitored student attentiveness and comprehension throughout and provided praise that encouraged continuous engagement. Your students benefited greatly from the warm and welcoming atmosphere you provided at every step of the lesson.

This teacher was working with all gates flung wide open. She constantly called forth the best results by guiding students through the difficult portions. A variety of activities and instructional methods gave students the freedom to learn in different modes. Their successes, even those associated with correcting errors, generated a positivity that flooded the room. Her performance was rated as Excellent.

An assessment of a fourth-grade English unit called out sturdy performance:

> You provided individual attention when and where needed. You praised students for their efforts and accomplishments. You did an excellent job explaining the lesson content and then allowed students to reinforce their knowledge by calling on them for additional explanations.

This teacher had a strong grasp of student feedback. She used several opportunities to engage and commend students, resulting in a rating of Satisfactory.

An elementary classroom's math unit observation resulted in these comments:

> You varied the teaching methods, but a variety of hands-on or more interactive assignments would greatly enhance student engagement. Students might also benefit from seeing their work posted.

In this case, the instructor needed to initiate more student feedback. There were moments when terms were rephrased, but they were based entirely on student questions and provided entirely by the teacher. While the guidance was sufficient, students were not provided with many opportunities to actively participate. This rating was therefore ranked as Needs Improvement.

A third-grade language arts class observation garnered this appraisal:

> Work on relating lesson content to previous and/or future learning. The questions posed throughout required only rote answers and were not thought provoking. Please give attention to allowing students to participate more when they have new ideas or perspectives.

This teacher really struggled with the spur-of-the-moment thinking young students can demand. Guidance provided before the lesson was clear, but any need for assistance in the moment threw him off track. This inflexibility also meant that fresh perspectives and unique ideas from students were set aside quickly and not given the attention they deserved. The result was a rating of Unsatisfactory.

ENGAGEMENT

Engagement demonstrates learning; sparks passion; and links lessons to other subjects, the world outside of school, and even other classmates.

An appraisal of a kindergarten math unit sparkled with engagement:

> This was a well-orchestrated lesson! You started with a warm-up of the numbers one to twenty set to music. When students were seated on the floor, you stated the objectives for the lesson. You used visuals of the nine shapes to review and determine levels of retained knowledge. You caringly reminded students to raise their hands to be called on.
>
> You called students by name and sprinkled praises throughout. You asked probing questions. Each student presented his or her finished work to the class. Kudos for a job well done!

This teacher kept a very young group continuously engaged. By shifting activities and managing transitions, she ensured that the group remained focused on her and the lesson. Students were praised for their efforts, and the results of those efforts were shared with the class. The instructor created an environment in which engagement generated constant connection. Her performance was rated as Excellent.

A first-grade science unit observation found an environment that supported engagement:

> You led the lesson by having students repeat after you. The lesson content was related to students' experiences, thereby allowing them to personally involve themselves. You closed the lesson by allowing students to share with a partner what they had learned.

In this classroom, the teacher ensured that engagement connected students to the world outside the classroom. By allowing individuals to share learning in a direct and intimate way, she ensured that their engagement knit the class together. This performance was rated as Satisfactory.

An appraisal of a sixth-grade math class on multiplying decimals by whole numbers needed a little guidance:

> Do allow for more opportunities for engagement. Group assignments can connect students to their supportive peers. When you ask questions, strive for more meaningful answers.

This teacher was well prepared and exceptionally knowledgeable. She did not, however, allow for much engagement. There was also a distinct lack of in-class activity that could push students to go deeper. Her performance was rated as Needs Improvement.

During a third-grade math assessment, engagement was found to be lax:

> Vary the materials and methods used to deliver the lesson. Check in occasionally to ensure that all students are on track with the lesson's progress. Give equal attention to all group members. Incorporate the use of technology in ways that *enhance* instruction rather than confuse students.

This instructor failed repeatedly to engage. The lesson was delivered using a single methodology that did not allow students to do anything other than listen. Additionally, the instructor rarely asked questions so she couldn't connect with learners at any level. Her attention remained focused on a few students, which alienated the rest of the class. The technology she chose was too advanced, leading to confusion and further distancing the group from learning. The result was a rating of Unsatisfactory.

REFLECTIVE TEACHING

Reflective teaching involves self-observation, self-evaluation, research into different methodologies, and student feedback.

A visit to an eighth-grade math class resulted in these comments:

> I was very impressed with the details of your plan and your lesson delivery. You are a natural in the classroom! You planned comprehensively and provided materials and resources that were major contributors to the students' ability to clearly understand the Pythagorean Theorem.
>
> Your varied teaching strategies generated great interest and excitement for students. The use of the anticipatory set, the video, and the guided practice is a sign that you planned for the spectrum of learners.

At various moments, the observer could determine the amount of reflective teaching this instructor engaged. The lesson plan and the activities proved a foreknowledge of the various learning needs she would encounter. Every element of the materials and the variety of activities were demonstrative of a thoughtful approach to what might happen while she was teaching. This performance was rated as Excellent.

A fourth-grade math class was appraised at the expected level:

> The four students who worked at the table directly with the teacher showed a genuine interest in wanting to play the math learning games. Other students had the opportunity to engage in hands-on learning to aid their mastery of multiplication facts. I commend you for having materials prepared ahead of time and ready for quick retrieval as needed.

This teacher knew her class well enough to provide a small variety of specific activities that would engage the entire class productively. She connected the unit to prior learning, and because her materials were at hand, she was able to move forward the moment the entire class had mastered the information. Her performance was rated as Satisfactory.

An appraisal of a first-grade reading class found strong performance, with the need for a little guidance:

> You presented a credible review of the "sh" sound through picture boards and the use of the video. This helped to solidify the sound when it was found at the beginning and end of words. You engaged students in hands-on activities to aid their mastery of the "sh" blend. Rather than tell students what you want them to do, try demonstrating or modeling the expectations. I think you are on your way to growing into the educator you long to become.

Teachers must be able to determine when and how to model expectations. A first-grade class is going to need more modeling, especially with sounds that must be recognized in print. The guidance was intended as a specific tip that would also trigger a deeper self-evaluation into her techniques for this age range. Additionally, her review of the sound was credible but not particularly inspired. With a little push here and there, she could develop better habits and truly rise. At this point, she was ranked as Needs Improvement.

The appraisal for a fifth-grade language arts class revealed good intentions that failed to deliver:

> You prepared teaching aids and a comprehensive lesson plan. You monitored student progress and clearly valued the contributions of every student. You showed great confidence in presenting the lesson plan, but students still struggled.

Be mindful of the need to provide background information for the lesson. Link the day's lesson to prior learning at the start. Provide students with all the relevant details they need for comprehension. Select teaching aids that are child centered and relevant to the objective at hand. A closure will sum up the lesson's points and enhance mastery.

Throughout this lesson, the teacher seemed at ease and very confident in the class's ability to master the concepts. Despite the instructor's enthusiasm, students struggled to understand the lesson's objectives, let alone succeed at learning. The aids were not appropriate for their grade level and needed to focus more fully on the day's objectives. This performance sank to the rank of Unsatisfactory.

CONCLUSION

Teaching with rigor challenges students to think critically and to achieve ever greater academic success. It triggers curiosity, a love of learning, and a broader perspective. A rigorous classroom environment encourages exploration and discovery. The appraisal considers how instructional methods, the investigation of student performance, engagement, and reflective teaching can enhance the classroom every day.

With only a few comments or notations, a principal can guide a teacher to higher performance. Reflective teaching methods can be discussed further in feedback sessions. Since teaching with rigor is tied so tightly to the students, the outsider's perspective can be invaluable for instructors at every level.

Chapter Eight

Teamsmanship

Teamsmanship, or the spirit of cooperation, is a core element for every teacher. By focusing on serving students, parents, and peers, teachers become high-functioning professionals who gain as much as they give. Being open to cooperating with every person at every level of their schools enhances the support teachers can provide.

Teachers who actively reach out find that benefits accrue to their own efforts. Their networks expand, and the expertise on which they can call grows exponentially. A respect for the administration and its needs ensures that daily tasks assist the school in reaching its goals. And in the classroom, the spirit of cooperation honors cultural diversity.

For teamsmanship, the four critical elements are:

- Rapport with students
- Rapport with parents
- Respect for the administration
- Respect for cultural diversity

Rapport with students involves building meaningful connections, engaging in genuine dialogue, encouraging a positive outlook on academic achievement, learning about and understanding the community from which students come, and an authentic approach.

Rapport with parents utilizes a variety of communication methods to connect with parents to keep them updated about activities and their child's progress, calls on parents to help address in-school issues, discovers how parents can get more involved, and discusses any needs parents have with their efforts to assist students.

Respect for the administration involves building and maintaining relationships with school administrators, staff, and peers; expressing gratitude for support; encouraging others to grow beyond their current level of achievement; adapting to the needs of others; and extending the same patience to others that they would like to receive.

Respect for cultural diversity recognizes how students' backgrounds shape their perspective, ensures that every communication conveys an open mindset, uses diverse teaching methods to reach students with different information acquisition and problem-solving skills, and deals with conflict in a sensitive way.

With the respect and warmth built through teamsmanship, teachers welcome students into classrooms that are comfortable, safe, and secure. They remove fears that differences will cause challenges, and they smooth the path to academic success. Students, parents, and peers know that the teacher is approachable. They become key players in a spirit of cooperation that strengthens the entire school.

Because teamsmanship can feel like a fuzzy goal for some people, the appraisal can provide quite a bit of assistance in building and strengthening these skills. Comments made during the appraisal or in feedback sessions afterward can include information on professional learning communities or peers who have something to offer.

Recommendations might also include how to enhance rapport with students. Calling out the ways a teacher recognizes and supports a student's background ensures that those patterns of behavior continue and that good practices are modeled for others. Cooperative learning methods not only allow students to help other students; they also encourage better rapport with those students. When beneficial activities are recognized by the administration, teachers expand the ways they implement those skills in the classroom.

RAPPORT WITH STUDENTS

Rapport supports meaningful connections, genuine dialogue, enthusiasm for academic success, an understanding of the community, and authenticity.

This second-grade reading class benefited from the teacher's approach to building rapport:

> Once again, you carried out your lesson with ease. I observed you make personal connections with your students to make the lesson memorable and transferable. You clearly communicated expectations for learning. You maintained a positive rapport with students. You provided help, support, and encouragement to all learners. You provided individual attention where needed.

> Students were attentive, and they responded immediately when you used the countdown. The confidence you exuded while teaching was amazing to observe. You showed enthusiasm for teaching, especially when you got down on the floor with students to make learning personal and up close.

This instructor clearly was a natural at connecting with her students. She ensured that information was provided in clear and concise ways that would help this age group understand and comply with instructions. Her activities enhanced connection when she moved to the same level as the students on the floor. Her energy and openness were conveyed, and every one of the students responded. Her performance was ranked as Excellent.

In a different second-grade classroom, a grammar unit displayed the teacher's growing strengths:

> I know a good teacher when I see one. You have the makings of a great teacher! I saw a confident teacher who exhibited patience. Your dedication to excellence and concern for students was felt. These are excellent qualities, so your path should only grow stronger.
>
> Your voice was strong, and students could easily see and hear you throughout the class. You self-corrected your mistake. You used a caring tone and offered words of encouragement for student responses. You called on volunteers and nonvolunteers alike. You used guided practice to illustrate student expectations with the mentor sentence.

This instructor clearly had a solid foundation in all the elements required for student rapport. With time, her abilities and skills would grow through encouragement from the administration and implementation of new techniques. Her performance was rated as Satisfactory.

A ninth-grade honors class in social studies had one weakness:

> Unfortunately, I didn't observe a lot of active teaching. The entire session was dedicated to group activities. Future classes need to utilize a variety of methods to ensure that the learning needs of all students are met. Implement methods that encourage students to build rapport with you so that they feel comfortable asking for assistance whenever the need arises.

Although an honors class can often be counted on to take steps on their own, teachers still need to be leaders. The guidance professional instructors provide is invaluable at every level of achievement. In this classroom, every student needed to feel that he or she could reach out for help. Only by building meaningful connections can that occur. This rating therefore was ranked as Needs Improvement.

This observation of a fifth-grade science class revealed other areas of concern:

> I would like to see you circulate around the classroom more and call on more students to ensure they are all with you. All students need to be given the opportunity to participate in the unit and interact with you.
>
> How is attendance taken? I didn't see this take place. You appeared to be nervous, and the atmosphere in the classroom was more one of a disciplinary leader rather than one who connects with students. A more positive attitude toward teaching and an environment that enables mutual respect would go far toward enabling academic excellence.

This teacher failed on multiple levels to connect. Student behaviors never got out of hand, but the general atmosphere was one of grudging compliance. This doesn't encourage a warm or open approach to learning, and the failure rested fully on the teacher's shoulders. This rating was Unsatisfactory.

RAPPORT WITH PARENTS

Rapport with parents varies communication methods, provides information, integrates support, and considers the needs of parents.

A visit to a third-grade math class revealed how understanding division can tie into elements outside the classroom and even call in parental involvement:

> Your lesson got off to an appropriate start with the math calendar. It was relevant to the experiences of third-graders. The lesson promoted student involvement. The lesson was hands-on, and students enjoyed the experience. The spark of delight when you passed out extra BrainPop sheets to take home and "quiz your parents" was a great moment! You connected class activities to their daily lives.

This teacher had a real knack for getting things done in unique ways. Instead of relying on only e-mails or other missives, this instructor used the students as a communication channel. The extra sheets provided a real example of the type of work their children performed. The fact that the sheet would be fun for the kids ensured that a majority of the parents would actually receive the information. This performance was rated as Excellent.

A third-grade language arts unit displayed the strengths of the teacher's parental outreach:

> You encouraged students to speak to their parents about how their jobs require the use of adjectives. The lesson reinforced skills using probing questions that linked the lesson plan to everyday activities. The lesson was made much more interesting due to this blend of activities and variety.

This teacher took what could have been a dry lesson and linked it to the worlds the students encountered outside of school. That allowed their learning to be linked to their family activities. It also was much more likely to allow parents to engage with their children about the lesson. This performance was rated as Satisfactory.

An observation of a third-grade reading and spelling class revealed many strengths with one weakness:

> Your lesson content was related to students' interests and life experiences. The lesson appealed to students and was appropriate for the curriculum and aligned to the goals of the lesson. I would like to see you utilize more real-world examples in the lessons. Particularly, encourage students to think about their lives outside of school when probing for comprehension. Consider assigning homework that encourages students to read aloud to a sibling or a parent to broaden the learning impact.

This teacher had the in-class components fairly well structured. Her enthusiasm was high, but she struggled with connecting the unit to real examples. The recommendation to include parents and other family members would serve academic goals while enhancing the school's connection with parents. This area was rated as Needs Improvement.

An assessment of a sixth-grade mathematics unit uncovered one critical flaw:

> You planned and implemented activities relevant to students' developmental levels. However, homework was not checked as a means of assuring mastery. When one student didn't turn in the assignment, he said that his parents had told him he didn't have to do the at-home assignments because they were never checked.
>
> This student's comment was overheard by the entire class. Your response did not clarify for students why homework is important. With your own lack of effort about checking the assignments, the students didn't seem motivated to do the additional work.

Homework isn't an area where parents are constantly involved, but in this case, the connection was clear. At least one student had complained about the uncredited work to his parents, who had responded with an option that did not support academic growth. Because the teacher failed to treat the work as important and failed to address the issue when it arose, this area was rated as Unsatisfactory.

Chapter 8
RESPECT FOR THE ADMINISTRATION

Respect for the administration builds and maintains relationships at school, values support, encourages others, and is considerate of others' needs.

This kindergarten social studies unit on character traits displayed the teacher's respect for everyone at the school:

> You demonstrated a knowledge of the subject matter. You selected appropriate strategies and materials that promoted student engagement. You asked students to provide the character traits they expected to see from school principals, teachers, and cafeteria workers. This tied the lesson into their everyday world and demonstrated your clear regard for everyone who works here.

The way this teacher spoke about her fellow professionals demonstrated a deep respect for their efforts. In modeling gratitude for her peers and school staff, she conveyed that same feeling to her students. Combined with her activities outside of the classroom, this teacher achieved a performance rating of Excellent.

An observation of a second-grade math unit displayed a foundation of learning based on administrative support:

> You presented information in an appropriate sequence based on recipes used by cafeteria staff. You supported verbal directions using visual aids that were like equipment used in the cafeteria. You prepared containers that were relevant to the objective. You summarized learning and allowed students a voice as well.

This teacher also connected her lesson plan to a specific part of the school. She had prepared by visiting the cafeteria and looking at the containers they used. By selecting materials based on a real and relevant example, she demonstrated that she valued the contributions of all individuals in the school. Her performance was rated as Satisfactory.

A fourth-grade language arts class was typically strong except during one unexpected moment:

> When one student went off topic with his Internet search and pulled up unflattering photos of another teacher, your response addressed only the off-task behavior. Next time students disrespect another teacher, model your regard for fellow professionals by defining this type of behavior as unacceptable.

The teacher opted in this moment to ignore the core of the behavior and push only for compliance. Perhaps he was unprepared for this type of activity. Nevertheless, he should have demonstrated clear disapproval. The performance in this instance was rated as Needs Improvement.

This visit to a first-grade reading class started out well but quickly fell apart:

> You made use of a story that was appropriate for this age and that allowed for the lesson objectives to be demonstrated. Since the story was about a mean teacher, it was natural that students shared experiences with teachers they found too tough or just mean.
>
> However, the way you handled this information was unprofessional. By encouraging students to name names, you encouraged disrespect for your peers. The addition of your own comments about times you found one specific person to be less than friendly were inappropriate.

During this visit, it appeared that the teacher was trying too hard to connect with students. Offering up personal stories is a great way to build relationships, but in this case, she did so at the expense of her peer. This type of behavior doesn't model respect. Additionally, it was very likely that the stories she shared would be passed along to other students. This performance area was rated as Unacceptable.

RESPECT FOR CULTURAL DIVERSITY

Respect for cultural diversity recognizes students' backgrounds, conveys acceptance, utilizes diverse teaching methods, and deals sensitively with conflict.

During an observation of a ninth- through twelfth-grade algebra class, the teacher utilized several methods for her culturally diverse group:

> You seemed to have a grasp of how each of your students learns best. You used probing questions to help clarify learning. You showed fairness to all and a compassionate attitude. I like the way you walked students through each problem using a step-by-step approach.
>
> Through a variety of learning methods, all students were encouraged to become active learners. You varied your teaching methods to meet the diverse needs of the students. I observed a high degree of respect for the perspectives of a diverse group of students!

Because this teacher was aware of the individual needs of her students and the backgrounds from which they came, she could implement the types of learning activities that helped them most. A variety of methods kept everyone learning at the same level and allowed everyone to grasp the concepts in different ways. By respecting cultural diversity, she helped all her students succeed. The performance was rated as Excellent.

A visit to an eight-grade math class resulted in the following comments:

> The activities were kept congruent with the needs of your diverse learners, and the discussion of a treasure chest set the stage for the introduction of the lesson. You demonstrated a respect for students' perspectives by the oral discussion and the way the lesson was delivered. The lesson clearly met the stated instructional objective.

This teacher did everything that was expected to meet her students on their individual academic paths. Both the teaching methodologies and the rapport allowed her to connect with individuals. Her performance was rated as Satisfactory.

An appraisal of a seventh-grade science unit was fairly strong but needed a little intervention:

> Your instructional method was geared toward stimulating interest in today's lesson and reflected a child-centered approach to teaching. You used appropriate facial and physical behaviors, gestures, and language; you exhibited appropriate confidence and poise in working with students from a variety of backgrounds. Do, however, be aware of gender differences in some cultures, and call on girls even if they don't volunteer to answer a question.

This teacher was exemplary in most of the areas involved with academic excellence. The one blind spot was that some cultures habituate girls to be modest and quiet. The instructor needed to call more frequently on students who weren't volunteering to avoid drawing attention. This area was ranked as Needs Improvement.

A visit to a fifth-grade English class turned up some serious deficits in cultural respect:

> The lesson plan proposed to address a variety of forms of figurative language. The examples you shared didn't connect well with these students. Most often, you utilized a type of questioning that asked only for yes or no answers and that didn't provide students the opportunity to think before they responded.
>
> The students you called on individually and challenged to think critically could not respond to the challenge because the questions did not display sensitivity to their backgrounds. Students cannot respond to situations they have not experienced themselves.

The school in this case was in a county with an exceptionally low average income. The questions the teacher asked dealt with areas of life the students likely had never experienced. Although she was attempting to connect with students and challenged a few to go beyond simple answers, the students failed because the instructor failed to meet them where they lived. The performance was rated as Unsatisfactory.

CONCLUSION

Cooperation is a singularly important core element in teachers. Drawing together the students, parents, and peers around them, teachers are able to provide more support to the school community. They also reap benefits far beyond the ones they give so freely. Students feel welcomed and safe. Parents can reach out and connect with the people leading their child's academic achievement. They model best practices for peers and integrate well with the administration's efforts.

Appraisal comments and feedback sessions can strengthen and expand efforts that are already working well. Specific recommendations can build better practices and generate an upward spiral. And the principal knows that every student is being served in ways that create a brighter future for the students, the school, and the nation.

Chapter Nine

Administrative Duties

The administrative duties teachers perform in the classroom, as well as those performed during their preparatory periods, help schools run smoothly. Everything from taking attendance and grading papers to managing paraprofessionals feeds into record keeping and the data gathered for the school and the district's use.

Administrative duties also ensure that the curriculum aligns with state and federal mandates. Rules and regulations laid down by various agencies must be fulfilled in ways that meet specific goals and serve the students. Although tools and techniques are often provided, teachers have quite a bit of leeway in how they fulfill many of these critical tasks.

These duties break down into four primary divisions:

- Record keeping
- Paraprofessional management
- Grading system
- Adherence to state, district, and school rules and regulations

Record keeping involves grades, attendance, notes, and other reports associated with individual students; historical records for lesson plans; and the master calendar for the academic year.

Paraprofessional management includes direct supervision of any instruction students receive, providing lesson plans, developing a written job description for work performed inside the classroom, and creating an environment in which the paraprofessional can succeed.

Grading system duties include recording marks associated with specific assignments, tracking due dates, implementing different scales to fit different assignments, and selecting precise and fair methods for grade assignment.

Adherence to state, district, and school rules and regulations covers safety guidelines; state statutes associated with academic performance; federal mandates that impact education; and school rules, such as codes of conduct and dress codes.

By fulfilling these duties, teachers ensure academic success for their students and contribute to the district's performance. These tasks, which are associated with the infrastructure of their school, help build and maintain achievement at the highest level. In tending to the details, teachers become keystones in their communities and their students' lives.

When an observation takes place, principals have the opportunity to troubleshoot issues small and large. Although much of the assistance will arrive during additional feedback sessions, classroom visits provide the chance to observe the infrastructure in action. The active way teachers monitor students is revealed alongside the results of that monitoring.

RECORD KEEPING

Record keeping tracks grades, attendance, and student progress; compiles lesson plans; and implements a master academic calendar.

This visit to a fifth-grade writing class found a teacher whose record keeping had been integrated into every element of her methods:

> Once again, you wrote and delivered a good lesson. Your discussion and activities allowed students to build on their knowledge base to master writing bio-poems while providing the opportunity for individual student assessment. I saw close monitoring and good lesson pacing. The written assignment that was added to their folders created a historical record of their progress. The self-assessment opportunity for students to suggest the grade they should receive for the day's assignment provided every student with the opportunity to reflect on their his or her progress.

The teacher's approach was creative and easily implemented. With the ability to suggest their grade, students could assess their progress in a thoughtful manner. When the class received their actual grades from the teacher, they could compare the results and adjust their pathway. For this category, the rating was Excellent.

A fifth-grade science teacher displayed a strong foundation in this subcategory:

> You used appropriate methods to track student progress. You adhered to the time frame set for the lesson and developed a plan based on your master calendar. The subject matter was related to a real-world concern and promoted a greater understanding of microorganisms in our environment. At various

moments, you linked the day's lesson to prior curricula to strengthen the arc of continuous learning.

This class benefited from an instructor who had prepared a challenging master calendar, with informative individual units. Students were clearly engaged in part because the lesson plan was well structured. This performance was rated as Satisfactory.

An appraisal of a fourth-grade reading class found one area that needed work:

During reading time, you utilized materials and resources that supported the lesson objective, and you made learning relevant to students by considering their interest in baked goods. During the lesson, you checked for evidence of comprehension.

The lesson could have been more interesting had you used supplemental materials, such as props, charts, graphic organizers, and/or other teaching aids. These types of materials would also provide opportunities to track student progress in ways different from asking questions to ensure comprehension.

Some students don't respond well to verbal prompts because their learning preferences are based in other areas. By utilizing more visual elements and even a few hands-on activities, the teacher could have ensured comprehension and gone deeper into her assessment of individual performance. This area was therefore rated as Needs Improvement.

A visit to a mixed kindergarten and first-grade social studies unit revealed several issues:

The primary lesson was fact-filled, engaging, and interesting to this age group. Since the remaining elements weren't challenging enough, off-task behaviors disrupted the class before and after the primary lesson. Compile your attendance records for future mixed-grade units to reduce the time spent on this duty. Always create a lesson plan that integrates elements that will appeal to and challenge both grade levels. Select activities that have specific goals to enable individual student assessment.

This instructor was poorly prepared for a mixed-grade unit. Rather than utilizing a lesson that engaged both levels, she fell back on a program that was too basic. Students lost the opportunity to learn while she lost the opportunity to track academic advancement. The performance was rated as Unsatisfactory.

Chapter 9

PARAPROFESSIONAL MANAGEMENT

Paraprofessional management involves direct supervision and providing lesson plans, a job description for the classroom, and an environment that supports success.

This assessment was for a grade school class serving students with learning disabilities:

> The list of duties and responsibilities provided to the paraprofessional is comprehensive and detailed. Having her take over the routine tasks of attendance and calendar review freed you for short interactions with individual students. Your approach to guiding her was professional and collegial and ensured that mutual respect was modeled for the students. She also took on the individual assistance required by two students during the lesson, freeing you to focus on moving the entire classroom forward.

Teachers need to balance their legal responsibility for students' education with the assistance the paraprofessional can offer. This instructor developed an approach that extracted every bit of help from the paraprofessional. The rating was Excellent.

An eighth-grade language arts class benefited from sound management practices:

> Lesson plans were effectively written and provided to the paraprofessional ahead of time. You defined the lesson objectives in detail so that her support was always in sync with the final goals. You gave clear directions and explanations even when she forgot the order of steps she was expected to take.

This teacher had developed a professional and respectful connection with the paraprofessional. The materials provided a clear pathway for those supportive activities, and she kept the assistant on task. The performance was rated as Satisfactory.

A sixth-grade math unit appraisal uncovered one area of weakness:

> The lesson was well organized and comprehensively written. Instructional time could have been better managed by providing the paraprofessional with materials and lesson plans ahead of time. Providing instructions in the moment takes time away from teaching and disrupts the flow of learning.

While this teacher was utilizing the paraprofessional in all the right areas, her approach didn't allow the assistant to anticipate the next step. Time was lost as the teacher provided instructions for every new step. During the class period, those small units of lost time added up to a significant number. The performance was rated as Needs Improvement.

A visit to a first-grade social studies/writing unit revealed the need for several changes:

> Since materials and a lesson plan were not provided to the paraprofessional ahead of time, she was not aware that the materials at the end of the story were not meant to be read aloud. By interrupting her, the respect students hold for her might have been undermined.
>
> Lesson plans are important guides for you and her. Always have a plan available. Hand off more of the daily tasks to the paraprofessional to free up your time for teaching. Allow her to assist students during assignments to ensure that all learners are given the chance to advance.

The paraprofessional in this classroom was underutilized and spent most of her time standing quietly to one side. When she was asked to assist, the instructions she received were not detailed or clear enough to enable her to assist students fully. This teacher's performance was rated as Unsatisfactory.

GRADING SYSTEM

Grading system duties involve tracking due dates, implementing appropriate grading scales, recording grades, and fairness.

An assessment of a kindergarten language arts class found a high level of performance:

> Before the lesson began, you asked students to look at their score from the prior day on the behavior and performance chart. Students were given the opportunity to self-assess by counting sets of matching pairs they collected. At the end of the lesson, the behavior and performance chart was renewed by having the students place markers at the level they had achieved. The feedback was immediate and provided a method of grading that was fair and transparent.

This instructor utilized self-assessment and group feedback to encourage engagement. Since the students knew immediately how they had performed, they were able to move forward with the goal of either maintaining a high score or improving their score. The system was beneficial and well integrated. The performance rating was Excellent.

A fifth-grade science unit garnered a strong appraisal:

> Students were led through an excellent recall exercise on the differences between a physical and chemical change along with identifying the properties of each. An appropriate data sheet was used to document learning. Learning was assessed via observation and the answers written on the data sheet.

This teacher used the sheets provided for the lesson to monitor performance. Having the students file the sheets in their individual folders built a historical record. This performance was rated as Satisfactory.

An appraisal of a first-grade reading lesson worked fairly well but missed one goal:

> Circulated throughout the room to monitor students' work. Planned a child-centered lesson that involved measurable outcomes. The final product, a fill-in-the-blank exercise, was not collected at the lesson's end. In the future, compile the tangible results to track performance and set grades.

Although this teacher did collect other work completed by the students, those assignments were not directly associated with the core lesson plan. She therefore lost the opportunity to compile data associated with the lesson's objectives and mandated standards. The performance was rated as Needs Improvement.

A visit to a fourth-grade social studies class uncovered a variety of flaws:

> Attention to details involved with the activity were scattered, resulting in confusion among students about how to undertake the activity. This resulted in a rushed approach to the lesson and an incomplete ability to assess academic performance. Organizational skills inside the classroom need attention!

Although the selection of materials and lessons fit the mandates and the age range well, this teacher had difficulty implementing in-class activities in an organized and efficient way. The approach left students confused and resulted in lost time. Because several students had to rush to finish the assignment, their grades likely would not result in accurate assessments. This performance was rated as Unsatisfactory.

ADHERENCE TO RULES AND REGULATIONS

Adherence to state, district, and school rules and regulations considers safety guidelines and regulations, state statutes, federal mandates, and school rules.

A visit to a first-grade science class revealed mastery in this category:

> You wrote a plan that was clearly aligned to the mandates associated with this grade level. The lesson challenged students to think critically. Students were excited to participate in learning about magnets in meaningful and creative ways. By modeling the expected activity, you ensured that the materials would be used in a safe manner. The class responded well to the clapping of hands used to get their attention. You guided students through the steps to achieve the lesson well.

This teacher had implemented a variety of methods to guide her students efficiently and safely through the activity. The lesson plan and her modeling of expected activity ensured that students remained on target for the mandated curricular goals. When necessary, she reminded the class of the rules governing their behavior and achieved immediate compliance. Her performance was ranked as Excellent.

A kindergarten reading class resulted in the following appraisal comments:

> You prepared a variety of appropriate supplemental materials to support the phonics lesson and meet educational mandates. You utilized varied teaching strategies to motivate students to achieve the expected academic advancement. There were clear directions and relevant examples.

This teacher achieved the goals associated with educational mandates with this lesson plan. Varied methodologies and appropriate materials ensured that these students would perform at the expected level. The performance was rated as Satisfactory.

A second-grade science class appraisal noted one area for improvement:

> The lesson was made more interesting using the supplemental materials supplied to the class as references. Your opening captured the interest of the students. The lesson clearly met the stated instructional objective. The lesson itself fell short in meeting all educational mandates. A broader approach in the reference materials and the lesson plan will ensure that students meet expected educational goals.

This teacher had prepared a great number of supplemental materials and provided a reference sheet but still fell short of expectations. Her materials were not broad enough to encompass all mandates, so the performance resulted in a rating of Needs Improvement.

A visit to a third-grade reading arts unit provided some much-needed intervention:

> The opening activity, although interesting, did not relate well to the lesson. A concrete framework for the lesson was not provided. You drew on your considerable knowledge and resource base to enhance learning with twenty-six examples. The examples ranged significantly outside of the stated intention of the day's lesson. Many also failed to support or return to state mandates.

Although this teacher was clearly trying to challenge his students, his efforts were unproductive. The disconnect between the opening activity and the lesson's goals didn't prepare students for the work. Many of the examples were only weakly linked to the curriculum. Although students were engaged in what they heard, they were not advancing toward mandated goals. This performance was rated as Unsatisfactory.

CONCLUSION

The administrative duties assigned to every teacher cover details small and large. By performing these tasks, teachers ensure that the school can successfully fulfill state and federal mandates, maintain a safe environment, and serve every student. Record keeping, paraprofessional management, grading, and regulation compliance build a system that runs smoothly.

Assessments can enhance the teacher's approach to and performance of these duties. Students walk a wider path to academic success. The district is more easily able to achieve its performance objectives. The community benefits immediately and well into the future as graduates begin their adult lives. By watching for signs of effective administration, principals ensure that even the smallest detail supports the complex edifice of education.

Chapter Ten

Instruction

Instruction is clearly the core of a teacher's career. A teacher's methods and approach must consistently achieve effective learning results despite the complexity of an ever-changing classroom . . . and even an ever-changing school and community environment. Since success can be negatively affected by the increasing pressures on the educational system as a whole, adapting instruction to meet these elements is a constant requirement.

This particular duty is impacted by some of the most wide-ranging elements involved in teaching. Instructors who recognize the essential elements become more effective because their decisions are based on the best techniques available in the moment. Everything from setting appropriate objectives to pivoting toward better options is involved.

The four elements to focus on for appraisals are:

- Assessment
- Technology
- Cocurricular activities
- Differentiated instruction

Assessment moves beyond the grades to determine how well individual students are achieving specific learning goals, uses evidence-based systems to assess students, and applies that knowledge to improve performance results for all students.

Technology includes all the equipment available in the classroom and using that equipment to enhance learning, engage and empower students, and allow for alternative teaching and learning methods.

Cocurricular activities complement academic goals by providing learning experiences that mirror the lesson plan, enhance a student's personal development, and allow for personal expression.

Differentiated instruction provides a variety of learning avenues that allow for different preferences and skill levels, develops lesson plans that provide access to all students, and varies the methods through which students engage in lessons.

These four areas add up to a core competency that generates an immediate impact. Together, they push students to reach their utmost level of performance and to engage in learning outside the classroom. A teacher who excels at instruction benefits individual students and their communities and districts for decades to come.

Because of the long-range and expansive impact of instructional excellence, appraisals play an important role. During assessments, principals spot areas where resources from outside the classroom can be pulled in to enhance success. An administrator's knowledge of family situations and challenges might adjust the trajectory of an individual's education and allow him or her to succeed despite the odds.

In terms of the teacher's performance, small comments can generate big benefits. Providing comparisons to other approaches can spur adjustments that create more efficiency. And when a principal discovers a method that works exceptionally well, that information can be passed along to other instructors.

ASSESSMENT

Assessment determines student learning, uses evidence-based systems, and ensures that all students meet performance expectations.

An appraisal of a first-grade language arts class found a teacher constantly in contact with students:

> This teacher clearly communicated expectations for learning and modeled the expectations. She posed questions that required open-ended thinking to allow students to demonstrate their level of learning. She encouraged students to participate actively during the delivery of the lesson to involve them in the curriculum in a direct manner.
>
> She provided help, support, and encouragement to all learners. She explained and reinforced the lesson content while aligning lesson activities with lesson objectives. The lesson plan provided measurable, evidence-based results.

This instructor performed so well because she implemented various methods to assess learning. In addition to the usual questions, she took students along with her while teaching the curriculum. Activities demonstrated specific points, which kept all the kids engaged and excited. It was as if she had found a way to allow the kids to teach themselves. Her performance was rated as Excellent.

A visit to a first-grade reading unit found a constellation of effective elements:

> You conducted an opening activity that established a framework for presenting a new skill: how to use a dictionary. Also, you utilized hands-on instructional materials that engaged students mentally and physically. You encouraged all students to participate in learning that was meaningful and creative, and you continuously monitored students' progress and adjusted when necessary.

This teacher's approach to instruction met all the expectations. The decisions she made about the lesson plan and activities supported students while allowing for individual monitoring. The hands-on portion provided opportunities for her to assist on a more personal basis and, when necessary, make changes that enhanced achievement. Her performance was rated as Satisfactory.

An observation of a fifth-grade writing class was excellent in many ways but needed one adjustment:

> Your enthusiasm for the subject seemed to have interfered with student learning. Individuals were given very little time to respond to questions, and at times, their in-depth comments were cut off before they could finish their thoughts. This in turn left little opportunity to assess individual learning or to signal when adjustments should be made for students who are struggling.

A motivated teacher is a true treasure! But even teachers have to know when to be quiet and allow students to take the floor. In this case, the instructor was bursting with ideas she wanted to share. Her desire to press on and provide ever more information left students without the opportunity to participate frequently enough for assessment to occur. Her performance in this area was rated Needs Improvement.

An appraisal of a first-grade math class uncovered a lower level of performance:

> Students were not encouraged to participate at any time in the lesson delivery. Questions were not directed to students, and when students raised their hands to ask a question on their own, they were not called on frequently. Little monitoring of student comprehension occurred.

This teacher was engaged much more with the curriculum than with the classroom. While a rich and deep understanding of the topic is important, instructors must be able to engage students in the moment. Without questions, participation, or activities, students were not monitored for comprehension except when their assignment sheets were graded after class. This performance was rated Unsatisfactory.

TECHNOLOGY

Technology considers available equipment and how that equipment is utilized for learning, engagement, and diverse learning preferences.

A twelfth-grade literature class was packed with appropriate and effective technologies:

> You infused technology into the lesson presentation. You encouraged students to share ideas and thoughts both inside the classroom and by posting tweets to the school's literature feed. You used an interactive activity in which students built a photo collage of images associated with the word "love" to pique interest in interpreting "Sonnet 43" by Elizabeth Barrett Browning.

This teacher clearly understood today's tech-savvy students. Her approach exceeded the requirement to utilize technology in the classroom and, in doing so, engaged every student by working with a constellation of digital options. Her performance was rated as Excellent.

An eighth-grade social studies observation resulted in the following comments:

> The teacher delivered a well-planned lesson from beginning to end! She infused technology in the supporting materials as well as the note-taking methods used by her students. The demonstrative PowerPoint presentation was on target for learning objectives.

Through careful preparation, this teacher implemented a variety of technologies that presented information in various formats. The technologies were all utilized according to their potential. Her performance was rated as Satisfactory.

A first-grade math unit went well enough until the technology failed:

> It was a real shame that the game you had planned to use wouldn't work. In the future, test game boards ahead of time, and keep spare batteries handy. Be sure to always have a backup plan for alternate activities in cases like this. The failure of a device shouldn't take the entire lesson off track.

While the teacher did eventually rebuild the students' enthusiasm, she hadn't planned an alternative that could replace the game. A little preparation would have kept from disappointing students and would have helped her move forward quickly. The performance in this case was rated as Needs Improvement.

A fifth-grade social studies unit faced a failure that couldn't be blamed on the technology:

> The technology selected should have enhanced understanding and provided enrichment. However, without even a basic grasp of how that technology functioned, students were constantly distracted by efforts to get the display to move to the next slide. Although they showed great patience, the overall effect was detrimental to learning goals.

In this case, the teacher had set up a program that integrated several types of media. Rather than using a single program that already had all the features loaded, he had cobbled together different programs. The presentation was marred with repeated failures of the different components to integrate with each other. Performance in this case was rated as Unacceptable.

COCURRICULAR ACTIVITIES

Cocurricular activities provide learning experiences that mirror lesson plans, enhance personal development, and allow for individual expression.

This eleventh-grade special education English/reading unit pulled cocurricular activities into the classroom to supercharge results:

> By encouraging students to write short skits at home that they acted out during this class time, the entire class was well behaved and remained focused on the work. I watched as you worked to engage all students in the presentation of each skit by assigning "helpers" to the student who was to perform next. The plan led to all the different elements working together.

This teacher took a unique approach to engage individuals who had been left behind by more formal educational approaches. The assignment generated a positive response and active participation. By utilizing a format that frequently is seen only in cocurricular activities, she tapped into the students' creativity and generated enthusiasm. The performance was rated as Excellent.

A seventh-grade science class benefited when the teacher based the lesson on the science fair:

> Your instructional method was geared toward stimulating interest in today's lesson and reflected a child-centered approach to teaching. Among other things, you kept the lesson moving by involving students in an in-class science fair. You had students get out of their seats and move from desk to desk to observe the results of their fellow students' efforts. Because you had students so active and engaged, they were well behaved.

Although only a handful of students in this class were involved with the science fair, this teacher drew connections to that activity inside her classroom. She replicated the fair's environment by having students set up an experiment, complete it, and then go around with notepads to make observations about other students' results. The idea was fresh, and it spurred students to think about why different teams produced different results. The performance was rated as Satisfactory.

An observation of a second-grade math unit had one recommendation:

> You provided a variety of learning experiences. More importantly, you allowed students to think beyond the limits of the textbook. You set high expectations for all learners, and you motivated students to achieve by introducing the need for math in cocurricular activities of interest to students. Do, however, take care not to allow the focus of the class to wander too far from the lesson plans when discussing cocurricular activities.

Students at this level are motivated by an eagerness to copy older students. The use of cocurricular examples led to many questions by the students about the extra activities and how they might participate. The focus turned too far away from academics, leading to a rating of Needs Improvement.

For a second-grade reading/literature class, the attempt at using cocurricular elements did not go well:

> You planned comprehensively and provided materials and activities that should have been major contributors to your students' ability to comprehend and retain information. The activity was too complex for this age range, however, leading to several off-task behaviours, as individual students required so much guidance during the activity.
>
> Instructional time was therefore not maximized, and the allotted schedule ran far over the set parameters. While I commend you for the attempt at utilizing an activity that required the participation of all the students, having them out of their seats and in different areas of the class at the same time led to too much disruption. The activity didn't go as planned, and learning goals were not met.

Because the teacher did not anticipate having to provide so much individual guidance during the activity, her diverted attention allowed the rest of the class to engage in off-task and poor behaviors. After a time, this led to a barely controlled activity that degraded further the longer it continued. The concept was good, but the selection of the material for the activity was far too ambitious for this grade level. The performance was rated as Unsatisfactory.

DIFFERENTIATED INSTRUCTION

Differentiated instruction serves different learning preferences and skill levels, provides academic access to all students, and varies the ways students engage with learning.

A visit to a kindergarten social studies unit uncovered a variety of differentiated techniques in action:

> The use of whiteboard technology presented images that were colorful and clear. Students could easily identify each community helper by the hats they wear. The use of proximity teaching along with a caring tone resulted in even the most reluctant learner participating.

> Usually IEP students have a hard time with change, but you transitioned from task to task in ways that were comfortable for this group. That comfort allowed you to implement a variety of teaching methods to achieve academic success for students with highly varied learning preferences and challenges. Kudos for a great job!

This teacher could have followed the usual protocol for dealing with IEP students and kept her approach on a singular track, but that would not have served students with such a distinct variety of learning preferences. She rose to the challenge by introducing each new step in a way that her students understood. The performance was rated as Excellent.

A visit to a second-grade reading class resulted in the following comments:

> You enhanced the lesson using appropriate learning aids, such as a PowerPoint presentation and a story quilt. Reading the story aloud and having students read portions and then locate the appropriate spot on the quilt worked well to integrate many forms of instruction.

This teacher integrated visual, auditory, and tactile elements into the lesson. She also kept students engaged with the quilt on a different level by having them point out the various parts of the story. This met differentiated instructional methods by using several sensory channels for teaching, so the performance was rated as Satisfactory.

An observation of a fourth-grade reading session was weak in only one area:

> You used a variety of teaching strategies to achieve the lesson objective. The students engaged in hands-on activities to aid in structuring mastery. You supported verbal directions with overhead visuals and excellent examples. The lesson went well; however, work on creating more extended activities for those who finish early.

The teacher achieved academic excellence for most students, using a diverse array of teaching methods. However, the hands-on activities were rapidly completed by students who were performing at the highest level. Because none of the activities were more challenging, these students sped through them with time to spare. They could have been engaged more with the addition of one or two activities that would have met their needs for higher academic challenges. This performance was rated as Needs Improvement.

A fifth-grade reading unit fell short on several points:

> Visuals need to be much clearer in terms of demonstrating the lesson's main points. Supplemental materials need to add quality to the lesson. Provide students with more creative and high-interest activities to stimulate learning. Utilize small groups to allow individuals working on higher and average comprehension and skill levels to work together on texts that challenge them rather than expecting them to sit idly while the ones most in need are given personal assistance.

Teachers have many opportunities to vary instructional methods, supplemental materials, and assignments to ensure that every student works on the skills they need to improve. In this case, the instructor did little to meet the needs of all students. Instead, the lesson plan met the needs only the lowest possible rubric, leaving much of the class uninspired and disengaged. The performance was rated as Unsatisfactory.

CONCLUSION

Instructional excellence is the goal of teachers' every effort. The methods they utilize in their lesson plans and their approach to academic engagement must mesh with the complexity of constant change. Being able to assess student performance, utilize appropriate technology, support cocurricular activities, and meet various learning needs are all part of the mix.

Assessments can strengthen this core competency by providing comments on what works and what needs adjustment. Teachers and students benefit by discovering new ways to achieve more. Consider how students are being assessed, the types of differentiated instructional methods, cocurricular elements, and the use of technology during the appraisal to generate top performance from every teacher.

Chapter Eleven

Pastoral Duties

The pastoral element of a teacher's role nurtures students' personal aspects. Largely ignored for much of the history of education, today's schools recognize the value of a supportive environment. In addition, strong relationships, pathways to personal fulfillment, and physical and psychological well-being are part of this focus.

When these elements align with instructional excellence, the result is a positive attitude toward school and learning, increased resiliency, better decision-making and risk-assessment skills, and enhanced confidence. All in all, pastoral care develops the personal, social, and academic components to create a well-rounded and happy student body.

The four areas that fall under pastoral duties are:

- Academic issues
- Encouragement
- Communication with peers, administration, and parents
- Extracurricular participation

Academic issues address factors such as learning challenges, physical disabilities or illness, and family situations and similar events that can negatively impact achievement.

Encouragement involves listening when students need to talk through their problems, providing referrals to appropriate support services, and acting as a role model to encourage positive personality traits.

Communication with peers, administration, and parents develops and maintains the connections between the teacher and these groups or individuals and ensures that each group or individual is provided with the information he or she needs in a timely manner.

Extracurricular participation encourages and supports the activities that further develop students' emotional, psychological, and physical well-being.

As these four core competencies make clear, pastoral care involves individuals, classrooms, schools, and community members. Because it actively integrates so many people and groups, quality pastoral care benefits students, educators, administrators, parents, and even citizens who have no direct connection to the school.

Appraisals can work on the ground to help teachers provide compassionate pastoral care. The same approach used for academic assessments under instruction can be used to determine student well-being. The record-keeping component of administrative duties provides data on attendance, behavior, and progress that can be harnessed for this duty.

During feedback sessions, principals can draw direct lines between what individual teachers do and how their activities support the school's strategic plans. By working with daily details as well as a broader view, the appraisal becomes a bridge that ties everything together to optimize the potential for success.

ACADEMIC ISSUES

When pastoral care is applied to academic issues, teachers ensure that learning challenges, physical difficulties, and events outside the classroom do not negatively impact educational achievement.

A visit to a sixth-grade science class resulted in the following comments:

> This was a TAG science class. During the lesson, the teacher served as a facilitator of learning for students who are self-motivated to learn. The classroom atmosphere was pleasant and friendly.

> I was particularly struck by the assistance provided to the deaf student. The approach was personal and warm and demonstrated an understanding of the student's needs. The teacher closely monitored all student progress during the group assignment and managed time effectively while counseling individuals. Exhibited patience, professionalism, and a positive attitude.

This instructor handled a variety of student needs. In addition to working with the deaf student, she also caught the struggles of another student who was unwilling to ask for assistance. The second student had experienced difficulties at home. A few minutes spent comforting that girl got her back on track and provided the comfort she needed in a safe environment. The performance was rated as Excellent.

A visit to an eleventh- and twelfth-grade social studies class resulted in the following comments:

> You had a good plan that was timely for high school students. You had great samples of advertising designed to sway the minds of the viewers. By supplying these images to the student with low vision for use on her laptop, you ensured that every student was given the same access to the supplementary materials.

This teacher took the steps needed to ensure that everything displayed on the AV equipment was provided in electronic form to a student with severe sight issues. The files were e-mailed to the student every morning so everything was ready the moment class began. This performance was rated as Satisfactory.

A fifth-grade math unit integrated the needs of all learners except in one area:

> In the future, be more aware of the difficulties some students have in moving to different areas of the classroom. The student who used a wheelchair had to navigate around several obstacles when called on to approach the whiteboard. There was no reason why the stack of new supplies had to be placed in a pathway that student needed to use, and his difficulty called undue attention to his physical challenges.

This teacher's single oversight might not have presented an issue for regularly abled students but for one who used a wheelchair, the careless placement of a few boxes turned into an embarrassment. This distracted the student from the assignment. The performance was rated as Needs Improvement.

An observation of a first-grade science class failed to accommodate one student with a temporary condition:

> You put together a wonderful lesson for curious first-graders. It is therefore very disappointing to note that the student wearing a cast was excluded from these activities. The need to utilize both hands during the activity meant that the student could only watch others. This could have been easily solved by pairing students for the activity and allowing them to split the different steps according to what this one individual could do.

Learning by doing is a powerful teaching tool. In this case, the student had been in a cast for a while, so the teacher could have planned for paired activities or even an activity that didn't require manipulation with two hands. The performance was rated as Unsatisfactory.

ENCOURAGEMENT

Encouragement involves listening to students' problems, providing service referrals, and acting as a role model.

An appraisal of a fourth-grade math session uncovered a true professional:

> She effectively utilized vivid voice inflections to generate excitement in students about the upcoming game activity. The lesson encouraged and achieved involvement at the highest level. She maintained a learning environment that contributed to a positive feeling of self-worth in the students. Individuals who struggled with the lesson's goals were given specific encouragement during the lesson presentation and in personal follow-up sessions while the class worked on the assignment.

This educational professional utilized various opportunities to provide encouragement. During class, praise and specific comments were provided. During short breaks before and after the unit, the teacher approached specific students and offered short yet detailed comments. This kind of nurturing exemplifies pastoral duties, and the performance was rated as Excellent.

The minutes before a fourth-grade math class presented an opportunity for pastoral care during this visit:

> As the class entered, one student lagged behind. She was clearly upset, and the teacher immediately responded. After taking her aside, the teacher listened and responded in a manner that was caring and not rushed despite the timing of the event. The student was referred to the counselor and excused from the class for that period.

This teacher knew her students well enough to spot a troubled child. Rather than allowing the girl to possibly lose the rest of her day to her emotional troubles, the instructor provided her with a pass so she could talk to the counselor. The performance was rated as Satisfactory.

An appraisal of a sixth-grade social studies class found one area that was lacking:

> Since the lesson plan was so ambitious, activities needed to move along rather quickly. When several students were unable to maintain that pace, your patience wore thin. This did not model positive traits for students and should be given more attention in the future.

In all other areas, this instructor performed exceptionally well. He monitored progress closely and provided praise and encouragement when things were going well. As time grew short, however, his patience with questions from a few students who were struggling didn't maintain an appropriate level. The performance was rated as Needs Improvement.

During a visit to a mixed second- and third-grade science class, a real issue arose:

> This was a whole-group session during which students were expected to work together. When two students began bickering, the disruption was allowed to get out of control because of the teacher's refusal to listen to the child who had been wronged. This led to an eruption in which students took sides and required quite a bit of time to bring under control.

This dramatic event could have been subdued much more quickly if the teacher had offered to take the distraught student aside and listen to her after the class had begun working on the activity. Instead, the teacher repeatedly said that she "didn't want to hear about it," which appeared unfair to the other students. The performance was rated as Unsatisfactory.

COMMUNICATION WITH OTHERS

Communication with peers, administration, and parents connects the teacher with other groups and individuals and ensures that appropriate information flows to those groups and individuals.

An appraisal for a first-grade writing class resulted in the following comments:

> You used good communication skills with the parents who were visiting, and you exhibited a cooperative and helpful approach when a teacher in the next classroom needed assistance. Despite these unusual events, time was effectively used, and you showed great enthusiasm for teaching. During the group activities, you provided individual attention to several students and their parents.

This teacher took the opportunity presented by an academic classroom visit to really connect with the parents. She integrated communications with the in-class activities and, when a teacher stopped in to ask for assistance, was able to provide help without disruption. This performance was rated as Excellent.

An observation of a third-grade math class began right after lunch:

> Before class started, a parent escorted her child to class after returning from a doctor's appointment. The parent's attempts to socialize were warmly accepted and, when chatting clearly was going to interfere with the prompt beginning of the class, you gently ended the conversation.

Teachers and parents interact many times and in various ways throughout the academic year. Good relationships are built and maintained by always providing a welcoming response, even if there isn't really time to engage in a discussion. In this case, the teacher called attention to the waiting class and her professional obligations to quickly end the conversation without alienating the parent. The performance was rated as Satisfactory.

A visit to a mixed-grade, high school writing class found one area that needed adjustment:

> The one area to work on is your response to one student's comments about another teacher. Rather than being clearly supportive of a peer, you provided a noncommittal answer that, in the minds of young adults, could have been misinterpreted as unsupportive. In the future, be sure to provide peers with every opportunity to be represented with respect by their coworkers.

This teacher in no way meant to undermine her peers, but as the comments note, children and young adults can misread nebulous statements. The recommendation to provide clearer responses in these matters drew her attention to a minor misstep that could have had consequences for that peer with these students. The performance was rated as Needs Improvement.

A fifth-grade social studies observation provided the opportunity to catch a negative situation evolving with a parent volunteer:

> Your lesson on understanding the Fourteenth Amendment had great potential; however, it left the observer wondering how familiar you are with the lesson information. While going over the answers to the quiz, you cited two answers that were incorrect.
>
> When the volunteer parent assisting the class pointed out the errors, your response was inappropriate. Rather than checking your information and thanking the adult for her acuity, you blamed the misinformation on the process by which the quiz answers were compiled. This undermined your relationship with the volunteer and did not model an appropriate maturity for students.

Clearly this teacher had a weak spot about being corrected even when it was done to ensure academic excellence. The inappropriate response also did not model positive personality traits, which undermined the instructor's relationship with both the students and the volunteer. This performance was rated as Unsatisfactory.

EXTRACURRICULAR PARTICIPATION

Encouraging students to participate in extracurricular activities helps develop their emotional, psychological, and physical well-being.

An assessment of a fourth-grade science class found plenty of these connections:

> You wrote a good plan that was aligned with the performance standards. To fulfill those goals, you called in the leader of the after-school science club. During her presentation, you utilized whiteboard technology to stimulate learning associated with her topic. After she left, the variety of activities and questions used to promote understanding were tied directly to her appearance. You planned a lesson that clearly motivated students to want to participate not only in the classroom activities but also in the after-school science club.

This instructor recognized that different individuals approach the same topic in different ways. She also knew that students often consider extracurricular activities to be more engaging than in-class units. She combined curricular goals with the appeal of an after-school program to supercharge this unit. The performance was rated as Excellent.

An observation of a kindergarten reading/phonics unit resulted in the following comments:

> You selected materials that supported the lesson objective and students' learning styles and pointed out which materials came from the school library's after-school story time. When students exhibited their enthusiasm for the extracurricular activity, you promised to provide that information on a sheet they could give to their parents.

This teacher recognized the value of extracurricular activities related to the unit and promised to supply relevant information. The performance was rated as Satisfactory.

A third-grade math class instructor could have made one small adjustment:

> It was immediately evident that you put a great deal of time and effort into today's lesson. Do take some time to learn exactly what the after-school math club does so you will be prepared for questions about participation next time they arise.

This teacher had the classroom environment under control. Everything was focused on moving students forward. However, when a student asked about the after-school math program, the instructor was unable to provide information about participating. This could have been resolved by offering to find out and get back to the class later. The performance was rated as Needs Improvement.

An appraisal of an eighth-grade language arts unit revealed deeper issues:

> You made learning fun, and you found innovative ways to challenge your students. However, when one student said she had already done the activity during an after-school book club, your response did not encourage other students to participate in that club. Expressing the idea that the leader of the book

club was "stealing your ideas" set up an adversarial component that might turn students loyal to you away from an enriching program.

While joking around is fine in class, this teacher's demeanor indicated she was not joking. She was clearly displeased by the overlapping components of the after-school activities with her classroom. Rather than applaud the overlap, she communicated the idea that the leader of the book club had done something wrong. The performance was rated as Unsatisfactory.

CONCLUSION

Pastoral duties develop students' ability to forge their own paths to personal fulfillment and psychological well-being. Additionally, they ensure that physical, developmental, or other challenges do not interfere with academic achievement.

Appraisals that consider this core competency address the teachers as well as every individual and group that benefits from quality pastoral care. Comments and feedback boost the ways teachers provide compassionate care in service of academic goals. The connections principals can draw between the classroom and the world outside the classroom broaden the road to complete success.

Chapter Twelve

Behavioral Competencies

For teachers, behavioral competencies are associated with their approach to their roles. Their choices and aptitudes in this area have a profound impact on students, peers, the school, and the community. A thoughtful approach must therefore encompass an understanding of how each choice might benefit these areas.

Because this duty is so intensely personal, all four of the subcategories can be considered subjectively as well as objectively. However, it begins with teachers' approach to education and their motivation and perspective on learning.

The four categories that make up this duty are:

- Creativity, adaptability, and flexibility
- Decision-making skills
- Problem solving
- Resilience and tenacity

Creativity, adaptability, and flexibility include changing course with and without notice, openly receiving feedback, and meeting challenges with unique solutions.

Decision-making skills utilize information from a variety of sources, apply a broad and multifaceted perspective to available options, consider outcomes and consequences, and then implement the steps involved with the final decision.

Problem solving involves a proactive approach to identifying issues, seeking solutions, considering the ramifications of alternatives, implementing a solution, and then evaluating the results.

Resilience and tenacity are the ability to continue in the face of challenges and to recover quickly after setbacks, self-efficacy, and unwavering dedication to professional and educational goals.

Taken together, these four categories are among the top required for the success of the teachers and their students and school. They are all qualities that seem to be inherent in the dedicated educational professional, and they are certainly required in the challenging environment of modern education.

Every one of these qualities is strengthened by being put into action. And that's where the appraisal process can be a significant source of assistance. Focusing on these areas communicates that teachers are not alone in their quest for improvement despite the odds. Knowing that the administration is actively involved goes a long way in enhancing morale on days when the classroom seems like an island.

Beyond these important motivational aspects, the appraisal can offer specific comments and detailed recommendations. Every note on an appraisal strengthens the growth mindset that powers these four elements. While teachers are the head cheerleaders for the students, during the evaluation process, the principal becomes both the instructor and the head cheerleader for behavioral competencies that matter so much.

CREATIVITY, ADAPTABILITY, AND FLEXIBILITY

Creativity, adaptability, and flexibility allow for necessary course adjustments, free-flowing feedback, and the resolution of challenges.

A kindergarten science class assessment uncovered several positive elements:

> The materials you selected fit the subject exceptionally well and ensured that the information was clear. You varied teaching strategies as needed to fit the ability of the different students. Because of that, you generated continuous excitement as students learned about the lesson's goals. You were observed conducting ongoing checks for comprehension. You pulled in an array of manipulative and hands-on aids to address the challenges of individual students, thereby reducing the need for the entire class to learn at a less-challenging level.

This instructor had thought through a variety of options and worked to resolve potential challenges before they arose. She could adjust on the fly to the needs of students operating at different skill levels, thereby using creative and unique solutions to serve the entire class. Her performance was rated as Excellent.

A visit to a second-grade math class disclosed a teacher resolving an unexpected challenge:

> The lesson on picture graphs utilized technology in an appropriate manner. When the file wouldn't load the last few supplemental materials, you shifted gears and asked the students to sketch the graphs you described and then drew the correct versions on the whiteboard, creating a fun and engaging activity out of a challenge.

This instructor quickly adjusted course when the supplemental materials suddenly became unavailable. Instead of floundering around for printed versions, she had the students create their own. Her performance was rated as Satisfactory.

A ninth-grade social studies unit appraisal offered the following comments:

> The way students answered the questions could have been more varied. Most questions were posed in a "What do you think?" format. In the future, ask more detailed questions to better guide students. This will keep them aligned with the curricular goals.

While this teacher led a lively and engaging lesson, the open nature of the questions didn't allow them to function as well as they could have. By providing more variety and adapting the format of the questions to specific points, she could enhance how students considered the information. The performance was rated as Needs Improvement.

A visit to a fifth-grade writing class found some issues:

> Instructional materials were not geared well toward stimulating interest in poetry. In part, this was due to the use of the same short poem to demonstrate multiple curricular elements. A variety of poems listed in the textbook could have been used instead of spending so much time on a single piece.
>
> Additionally, the approach to teaching could have engaged students more directly. Rather than asking them to locate examples in only the text provided, they could have written their own short example. This was really a missed opportunity.

In cases where the lesson involves curriculum that students tend to consider difficult, it's especially important that teachers utilize creativity. And when the presentation of a lesson is so clearly failing to connect, teachers need to be able to shift their approach and locate new ways to inspire learning. This performance was rated as Unsatisfactory.

DECISION-MAKING SKILLS

Decision-making skills utilize broad information sources, locate options, consider outcomes, and implement the final decision.

An observation of a fifth-grade science lab resonated with good decision-making skills:

> Even the title of this unit, the Elephant Toothpaste Lab, inspired engagement. Your selection of different apps for use during the lab meets the demands for the highly skilled professional approach required in today's classrooms. Your students benefit from your preparedness, your attention to science details, and the effort you put into researching and implementing new resources not found in other classrooms.

This instructor clearly pulled in all the components of an educational professional when deciding how to teach a particular unit. The unique elements she selected from the available programs were engaging and raised her efforts above those of others. The performance was rated as Excellent.

An observation of a first-grade math unit reflected on decision-making skills:

> From reading your plan, I can see that you put a lot of thought into creating and delivering a lesson that would meet the requirements for the day. During the lesson, students were required to speak, read, and write information related to the lesson. The decisions you made about which materials to use challenged students to perform by engaging them in activities that served to support and assist with lesson mastery.

The instructor founded her decisions on a broad array of available options, and she considered the outcomes. She met mandates and provided her class with a strong foundational knowledge. The performance was rated as Satisfactory.

An appraisal of a first-grade social studies unit offered one recommendation:

> Overall your lesson plan was balanced, and you utilized a tangible teaching aid to stimulate interest in the topic. You might pull in more technology for future lesson plans. Particularly with a topic like goods and services, a host of options are available for your consideration even at this young level.

The teacher met the mandates through her lesson plan but could have enhanced the experience as well as the learning results by utilizing technology. This especially applied to her approach, which offered a variety of real-world elements that could have triggered deeper student engagement. The performance was rated as Needs Improvement.

An appraisal of a first-grade language arts class showed the need for better decision making:

> Students were called to the carpet in an orderly manner so they could participate in a hands-on activity. Several students exhibited poor behavior during the transition and continued acting up during the activity. They were reminded of expected behaviors, and when they failed, they were asked to move their reward pin down the chart.
>
> One of these students refused to engage in the reward chart activity, so you moved the pin for him. This did not result in the desired impact, and the student continued to act out. Subsequent movements of the pin also had no impact. The approach for this student's behaviors needs to be changed so the class is not continually disrupted.

This teacher failed to determine the best way to deal with uncooperative and negative behavior. The approach failed time after time, so she needed to shift tactics. Follow-up with the instructor revealed a lack of ability to make decisions inside the classroom in areas relating to negative behaviors with all students; she preferred to take time after class and think through the events before deciding. The rating was marked as Unsatisfactory.

PROBLEM SOLVING

Problem solving involves proactively identifying issues, seeking out and implementing solutions, and evaluating results.

An observation of a third-grade science class provided an opportunity to watch problem solving in action:

> A student's angry outburst was met with a calm attitude. Although she lashed out at you personally, you did not react to that attack. Instead, you asked her to approach your desk while you settled the rest of the class in their activity. Then you privately spoke to the angry student and worked with her to locate a solution.

This teacher remained calm and steady in the face of a distraught student. She took appropriate steps to deal with the in-class situation. Additionally, she guided the student toward a resolution. The performance was rated as Excellent.

This visit to a mixed-grade science class revealed a teacher who exercised a variety of tactics:

> During this observation, the focus of my attention was on classroom management. Prior observations had revealed difficulties with management and discipline, and you were asked to implement changes to address these issues.
>
> You got students' attention before beginning the lesson. Students raised their hands and waited to be acknowledged before answering questions. I observed

> that some students' seats had changed since my last visit. This allowed you to proceed with classroom routines without a loss of significant instructional time.
>
> You used assertive discipline strategies to calm the classroom when necessary. You scanned the room to encourage appropriate behaviors and to redirect off-task behavior. Kudos for the positive changes that I observed today!

During prior observations, the instructor had not managed to control off-task and negative behaviors. After receiving feedback, the teacher implemented steps to solve the problems. The performance was rated as Satisfactory.

In a third-grade reading/language arts class, problem solving could have been more appropriately designed:

> You monitored students' attentiveness throughout and noted the continual pouting of one student who constantly refused to participate in class or work on the group activity. After attempts to redirect her attention, you ended by scolding her for her behavior.
>
> It would be better to listen to the student to get to the real issue or to help her express her frustration in a more appropriate manner. In the future, try not to exacerbate a bad situation by drawing attention to this type of behavior through public scolding.

When children present volatile emotions, a calm and capable approach is required. This instructor allowed her frustration to get out of hand, which resulted in a scolding that was inappropriate for the situation. The performance was rated as Needs Improvement.

During a fourth-grade math class, the teacher needed better problem-solving skills:

> In this class, the same student was acting disrespectfully to several of his peers. He repeatedly called individuals who gave incorrect or incomplete answers "stupid," and when the time came for group activities, he pulled the chair out from under another student as she sat down.
>
> Your response was lacking in corrective disciplinary methods. After telling the student to be kind to others, you should have clearly indicated that such behavior is not allowed in your classroom. Consequences need to be applied for continued disruptions. Pulling out the chair should have resulted in immediate action, such as removing the student from class.

This teacher had one way of dealing with negative behaviors, and it was appropriate for only very mild infractions. She needed to learn a variety of ways to solve issues. Relying on a student's conscience wasn't getting her anywhere, and she lacked the ability to modify her response. The performance was rated as Unsatisfactory.

RESILIENCE AND TENACITY

Resilience and tenacity enable continuous effort, a speedy recovery from setbacks, self-efficacy, and unwavering dedication.

An observation of a grade school resource math class discovered the need for quite a bit of resilience:

> Upon arrival, I observed you handling things very well. This group of students was particularly challenging because they presented a wide variety of skill levels. You varied the teaching methods to meet diverse math needs. You also changed methods as the lesson progressed in response to specific difficulties encountered by two students.
>
> The student conflicts that arose were corrected with care. When one conflict arose multiple times, you persisted in your patient and nurturing approach, and you continued changing tactics until you found the method that resolved the conflict.

This teacher continuously maintained a warm and professional demeanor. Because she was so unflappable, she could continue searching for new pathways for individual students who presented particularly strong challenges. The performance was rated as Excellent.

A third-grade language arts class appraised with a special focus on classroom management found a teacher who displayed dedication and tenacity:

> You provided clear directions and relevant examples. Your response to classroom issues was accurate and timely. You corrected students' behaviors with patience. You made liberal use of words of approval and assurance. You exhibited a dedication to resolving issues and a positive attitude.

This teacher had addressed areas that needed improvement to lift his performance, and the results were clear. The performance was rated as Satisfactory.

An appraisal of a third-grade reading class focused on areas that in prior observations had been marked for improvement:

> You planned and implemented activities relevant to the students' developmental level. You posed thought-provoking questions specific to the skills being taught. You gave timely and helpful feedback. Many of the areas of weakness have been brought up to the expected level. You have demonstrated impressive professional growth since commencing with teaching!

> I would, however, still like to see you include more variety in your lesson plans. Vary the methods of instruction to promote the students' interest and engagement.

This teacher was performing well in most areas but still needed to focus on engagement. The weakness had been brought forward before, so more persistence was required. The rating was marked as Needs Improvement.

A visit to a kindergarten reading class appraised a teacher who fell short:

> You used a caring and encouraging tone when addressing the entire class and while first responding to students who had trouble grasping the review and the new material. Individual attention was not provided every time it was needed. Again, you stopped providing support when certain students struggled with letters.
>
> Persistence is necessary, especially when dealing with a very young age group. Support must be continuous. The rest of the class was engaged and well behaved, so there was no reason the struggling student could not have been given more personal attention.

This instructor gave up too easily on one student. A host of remedies were available, and it might have been appropriate to refer this child for testing for learning challenges. Without the application of determined assistance, the student was not being served. The performance was rated as Unsatisfactory.

CONCLUSION

Behavioral competencies impact so much of a teacher's role. Peers, parents, students, and the school benefit from a thoughtful approach. The four subcategories associated with this duty are required for professional and academic success. Every one of these qualities grows stronger when they are practiced in the classroom and when the results are reflected on by the teacher and during the appraisal process.

Specific comments and detailed recommendations enhance the attitude that underlies behavioral competencies. An important extra benefit of the appraisal is that teachers gain a new perspective on how they implement effort associated with these categories. Their results improve in the classroom, and they grow more quickly into the high-quality instructors everyone wants at their school.

Chapter Thirteen

Teacher as Leader

Teachers lead in a variety of ways. They guide students through the challenges of academic achievement toward a lifetime of curiosity and engaged learning. As part of this, they function as instructional specialists, curriculum experts, and resource providers. They facilitate learning, mentor young minds, and mold the personalities of the people in their care.

Teachers can also become leaders among their peers. They model best practices and professional attitudes that impact the school's atmosphere. They help parents locate the resources families need to support education. At their best, teachers who are leaders become shining beacons of excellence that can transform a community and its view of a school.

The four areas associated with teacher leadership are:

- Modeling lifelong learning
- Collaborative teaching and learning
- System support
- Mentoring

Modeling lifelong learning includes guiding students toward resources where they can learn on their own, sharing their interest in taking classes or visiting institutions where learning can take place and encouraging new approaches to learning.

Collaborative teaching and learning provides small- and large-group activities, implements peer-to-peer learning and feedback, and involves other individuals as co-teachers.

System support includes participation in problem solving of school-wide issues, helping to build and participating in an inclusive school culture, and involvement in a collaborative infrastructure.

Mentoring empowers and supports new teachers, assists individuals who require support on a temporary (short- or long-term) basis, and shares best practices with peers.

Within these four areas, teachers will exhibit a variety of leadership tactics. Some will implement formal programs inside their classrooms to address individual student issues or to enhance learning for all students. Others will work informally with peers or parents and yet still be very active leaders. No matter how they approach leadership, teachers help shape the school's culture, and they have a direct impact.

The appraisal process is a perfect vehicle to support and develop leadership among teachers. Comments and recommendations trigger change that is powerful and positive. The ability of the principal to connect one teacher with others, to share a different approach, and to point the way to new resources is one of the primary benefits that can come from an observation. Best of all, a teacher leader discovered during the appraisal can become a new resource for peers, parents, and other students.

MODELING LIFELONG LEARNING

By modeling lifelong learning, teachers guide students toward information and educational resources, demonstrate their interest in personal academic goals, and encourage new educational pathways.

This kindergarten math class evaluated the performance of a teacher dedicated to modeling lifelong learning:

> This was a well-orchestrated unit on shapes. The lesson followed an organized sequence with every step introduced by your own experience with understanding shapes. You even pulled your set of keys out of your desk to show students the different shapes of the keys and described how each shape related to a different lock in your home.

> Modeling how you use the information every day helped set the tone for the guided practice to go well. It also encouraged students to engage with information they knew would be relevant to their own world and displayed a love of continual learning.

This teacher took every opportunity to engage young minds with a love of learning that would serve them their entire lives. Even something as basic as understanding shapes became an opportunity for the teacher to relate the lesson to her use of the information in everyday life. The performance was rated as Excellent.

A kindergarten social studies unit was evaluated with the following results:

> You related the lesson content to students' daily experiences. You clearly explained the lesson objectives and learning tasks and discussed why an understanding of the American flag is important.

During this unit, the class was given a variety of reasons why they should know about the American flag. They were also encouraged to provide their own reasons why it might be important. The connection between the curriculum and their daily lives encouraged lifelong learning. The performance was rated as Satisfactory.

A sixth-grade mathematics class assessment turned up one area for improvement:

> You planned and implemented activities relevant to students' developmental levels. However, this unit on ratios and rates was a prime opportunity to relate the lesson to students' lives. Nothing was presented about why skills in these areas might be useful to students right away, so this was a missed opportunity.

The instructor had many strengths but tended to teach along a very narrow range. There were multiple opportunities for her to connect the classwork with areas where students might need this information, so encouraging the pursuit of information and learning outside the classroom was missed. The performance was rated as Needs Improvement.

An appraisal of a fourth-grade writing unit resulted in these comments:

> Your background in writing is broad and diverse. It was therefore disappointing to find that you don't share your experiences with students. When they don't hear about how you apply these lessons in your own work, they fail to understand that writing is applicable in areas outside the classroom.
>
> As a teacher, you are the expert in this subject matter. You really do have a duty to provide everything you know to students to encourage their continual pursuit of excellence. By sticking so closely to the textbook, you do a disservice to this class.

Although the teacher might not have wanted to share personal details in class, she could have talked about how different types of writing are important in the broader world. She could have drawn on the careers of other authors or reporters to make this connection but did not. The performance was rated as Unsatisfactory.

COLLABORATIVE TEACHING AND LEARNING

Collaborative teaching and learning implement group activities and peer-to-peer interchanges for students and involve other teachers when possible.

A visit to a kindergarten math class demonstrated a variety of methods that worked:

> The skip-counting whole-class activity helped students make connections between what they know about counting. The linking-numbers activity you set up for small groups promoted maximum participation. It allowed for thinking and doing to occur simultaneously. In addition, it promoted using cooperative skills. Students presented their finished work in pairs. This helped to stimulate the fun in producing good work and provided the opportunity for students to help each other.

This teacher utilized multiple activities so students could work with each other on various tasks. Her performance was rated as Excellent.

This sixth-grade math class assessment uncovered a fundamental approach:

> You implemented a plan that included hands-on and group work to solve problems. Your directions to the leaders of each small group were clear and placed peer-to-peer assistance in the hands of the students.

In this case, the teacher set up a group activity that allowed students to work together. She also had one student from each group prompt others for feedback on individual efforts to ensure that every child received comments. The performance was rated as Satisfactory.

A kindergarten language arts unit assessment resulted in the following comments:

> You required students to write and planned activities that were appropriate for the lesson. The one activity that seemed a natural fit was missing, however. You could have asked students to read their sentences aloud, or they could have formed into groups based on the recess-related words they chose. In the future, find ways for students to interact with each other and help each other excel.

This unit engaged students fairly well but could have been enhanced by allowing students to help each other. The performance was rated as Needs Improvement.

A third-grade math unit assessment pinpointed several elements that failed:

> Work on using a variety of approaches to deliver instruction. In particular, allow groups enough time to finish the assignment. Give equal attention to all groups and group members. Ensure that group assignments require interactions between students to take full advantage of the approach. Assigning problems that can be individually solved doesn't require interaction.

Although the teacher attempted to utilize group activities, the assignment given for the groups really wasn't suited to the task. Students ended up working on the problems by themselves and didn't interact with each other. The performance was rated as Unsatisfactory.

SYSTEM SUPPORT

System support involves school-wide problem solving, participation in the school's culture, cross-subject integration, and supporting a collaborative infrastructure.

An assessment of a fourth-grade language arts class resulted in these comments:

> Learning was made relevant by considering the interests of students. I especially liked the energy and excitement generated by students playing Ball Hog. All students appeared engaged and eager to partner and play the game using their synonym, antonym, and homonym cards. Each trump by a student required him or her to note one other curricular subject where the word could be used and to provide a sentence using that word before play could continue. You planned a good lesson that reached into other areas to support the day's learning.

This teacher's efforts resulted in a fast-moving class that kept students thinking ahead. They knew they were going to have to make a connection to other classes, so even when their turn didn't result in a trump, they were still making these cross-subject connections in their minds. The performance was rated as Excellent.

A visit to a first-grade language arts class resulted in the following observations:

> The materials were prepared ahead of time and were borrowed from other curricular areas to spark a variety of ideas. Students were eager to share their "I can" statements, and because of the materials, they often talked about other subject areas.

By utilizing items borrowed from other classrooms, the teacher found a way to naturally integrate cross-subject elements. The performance was rated as Satisfactory.

A different first-grade language arts unit fell short of supporting the school's implementation of core curriculum components:

> The lesson was connected to prior learning, providing transfer knowledge to establish the basis for today's lesson. However, the unit did not integrate the new approach for plurals. In the future, pay attention to these mandates.

Since the mandates were new, this teacher's failure to utilize them might have been simply an oversight. A single note was enough to correct the issue going forward. The performance was rated as Needs Improvement.

A fifth-grade reading unit assessment located issues with peer-to-peer assistance:

> You showed evidence of good preparation for this lesson but did not integrate the components discussed in the latest reading collaborative group's recommendations. These concrete frameworks have been developed to improve education along the common themes in need of improvement school wide. A lot of effort has gone into analyzing student performance and techniques that can improve academic success. The administration is supportive of this endeavor.

Although a variety of suggestions had been made by the teacher-run reading collaborative group, this instructor did not integrate any of the recommendations. There was a complete lack of support for this school-wide effort, so the performance was rated as Unsatisfactory.

MENTORING

Mentoring empowers and supports new teachers and individuals who require more support on a temporary (short- or long-term) basis and shares best practices with peers.

A visit to an eighth-grade science/chemistry class revealed the following:

> Soon after class began, the new teacher in the next room stopped in to ask for assistance. You clearly explained how to solve the issue and provided a copy of the materials you use. This assistance was provided quickly and with minimal fuss, allowing the teacher to feel confident in knowing that support will always be available.

This instructor dealt efficiently and patiently with another teacher's request for assistance. Although the issue was not minor, the instructor being observed found a solution and quickly empowered the new teacher to proceed. The performance was rated as Excellent.

This evaluation of a fifth-grade science class considered a co-teaching situation:

> You delivered an impressive lesson on inherited traits versus environmental characteristics. It was exciting and engaging and allowed for an equal amount of teaching by both instructors. The teamwork supported best practices and ensured learning success.

In this case, a new teacher had been paired up with an experienced science instructor to meet the needs of a specific class. The two worked well together. The guidance provided by the more-experienced teacher led the way to academic achievement. The performance was rated as Satisfactory.

A fourth-grade math class observation found one area that needed attention:

> Students seemed eager to learn and were motivated. They also seemed happy to be taught by the new teacher. Her excellent rapport contributed to the enthusiasm for the learning they displayed. However, not all learners were within sight of you [the mentoring teacher], which allowed behaviors to get out of hand. When supporting a new teacher, keep in mind that instructional methods are not the only area where you might help.

In this case, the mentor could have provided more support for the new teacher by keeping a closer eye on the students. With time, the new teacher could have learned through observation how best to manage the entire classroom. The mentor's performance was rated as Needs Improvement.

In a kindergarten class that was co-taught, the mentoring fell far short of expectations:

> The class was not conducted in an environment that allowed for effective teaching or learning. Students' behaviors didn't support any of the delivery efforts, and the first-year teacher was left to her own devices to attempt classroom control. Instead of lending a hand, you spent the entire time compiling report cards as the new teacher struggled to teach and continuously tried to gain and maintain student attention.

In this instance, the co-teacher was ignoring the continuous duty that fell on both instructors to maintain an effective learning environment. Her lack of awareness or effort meant that the lesson was interrupted several times, resulting in poor performance for all students. The rating was marked as Unsatisfactory.

CONCLUSION

Teachers who lead help students surpass challenges and develop as lifelong learners. They model the attitudes, perspectives, and actions of true professionals. By excelling at their roles inside the classroom, they inspire and engage families and community members.

Whether their approach is formal or informal, involves participation in special focus groups or working solely on an individual level, they build an atmosphere of academic excellence. The appraisal can support and develop leadership traits. In the process, the evaluations become another tool for student growth, career success among educators, and a school that serves every member of its community by producing young adults who are ready for their roles in society.

III

Preformed Comments

Chapter Fourteen

Useful Comments

Because of the number of classrooms that must be visited in person during the appraisal process, efficiency is critical. And yet, if all that effort is going to be fruitful, the appraisal must provide detailed, effective comments. Every note and recommendation in an appraisal must be on target and speak directly to the core components under consideration.

This chapter provides you with a huge leap forward in both efficiency and effectiveness. The tables that follow provide ready-made comments that can be pasted into appraisals. Each table focuses on one of the ten key duties. The comments themselves are grouped under applicable performance tiers.

Use these tables to give teachers specific, actionable comments and pinpoint performance areas you wish to highlight. You'll provide a comprehensive list of items of note, support continuous quality, and guide individuals toward effective resolutions for problem areas.

Table 14.1. Professionalism

Conduct	**Excellent/Satisfactory**
	• Great teachers are the ones who care. • Great teachers settle for nothing less than excellence. • Great teachers prepare the launching pad for students to succeed. • You are making a difference in the educational life of every student. • You should be very proud of the way you present yourself as a teacher. • You exhibited the behavior of a masterful teacher. • You modeled caring, fairness, and enthusiasm for learning. • Students feel your belief in their potential to learn. • I was impressed at how well you handled the lesson. • Rather than make excuses for the things that didn't go well, you delivered a good lesson. • You created a classroom atmosphere that inspired students to academic success. • You encouraged all students in learning that was meaningful and creative. • I observed a lesson provided with strong methods that inspired students to learn and generated a powerful academic environment. • I was extremely impressed with the care you gave to the lesson.
Conduct	**Needs Attention/Unsatisfactory**
	• The exercise was not introduced. • Work on commanding students' attention. • Work on achieving cooperation from all students. • A more professional approach is required. • Make sure that students understand how much you truly care. • Students who raised their hands were not called on. • The teacher did not offer the assistance students needed. • Closure was not provided in a professional manner.
Mandates	**Excellent/Satisfactory**
	• The plan met the lesson's academic goals. • The materials you selected fit the subject exceptionally well. • The materials selected ensured that the information was clear. • Use of the overhead projector modeled for students as the lesson was delivered. • I observed good, sound, professional practices at work during a child-centered lesson. • You developed a unit plan congruent with state standards. • Sufficient time was allowed for students to practice the acquired skill. • Your students benefit from the way you plan your lessons. • You started with a well-developed plan.
Mandates	**Needs Attention/Unsatisfactory**
	• Adjust your teaching as needed whenever you check in with students to gauge their level of understanding.

- Strive to attentively assist students on an individual basis to ensure their needs are met.
- Provide sufficient time for students to write the required standard.
- Proof/check your lesson plan/materials for errors.
- Plans should always be available.
- A number of actions that could have added quality to the lesson were not performed.
- A number of activities that could have enhanced learner achievement were not offered.
- The visual aids/materials were unclear.
- The opening segment did not expose students to the lesson's objectives.
- The opening didn't anticipate academic success.

Interpersonal   Excellent/Satisfactory

- The lesson delivery reflected a child-centered approach.
- You maintained a professional demeanor throughout the lesson.
- You exhibited energy and enthusiasm.
- Your personal story was quite fitting for this lesson.
- You exhibited fairness and patience.
- You offered lots of praise and encouragement.
- You used a modulated tone of voice to lend excitement to the lesson.

Interpersonal   Needs Attention/Unsatisfactory

- Your delivery for the most part lacked strong confidence.
- I did not hear the lesson closure, which helps students organize the information into a meaningful context.
- Your demeanor must be professional at all times.
- Provide one-on-one assistance when needed.
- I have every confidence that you are going to be fine once you get over your nervousness.
- Remember to offer more words of encouragement for correct answers.
- Circulate throughout the classroom to ensure participation.
- Review strategies to use with uncooperative students.

Attitude   Excellent/Satisfactory

- You put together a plan that was energizing, fun, and captivating.
- You owned the room from start to finish.
- It was evident that you have achieved mastery in the classroom.
- You displayed energy and enthusiasm for teaching.
- You came across as someone who will work tirelessly to ensure that all students will be effectively taught.
- You planned activities in ways that made learning fun.
- You corrected inappropriate behaviors without disturbing the learning process.
- You exhibited a positive attitude.

Attitude	**Needs Attention/Unsatisfactory**
	• Trying to be friends with students never works in the classroom. • Work on demonstrating a more positive attitude. • Demonstrate a positive attitude toward teaching. • Always strive for students to respect you. • Consistently reinforce standards of classroom behavior. • Please show respect for all learners regardless of their current level of skill. • Use an appropriate tone of voice when addressing students. • Show more enthusiasm for learning.

Table 14.2. Planning and Preparation

Knowledge	**Excellent/Satisfactory**
	• You prepared in detail so your students could master the lesson. • You enthusiastically reached out to individual students to provide them with your knowledge. • I imagine that you spend countless hours searching for ways and ideas to enrich your lesson plans/lesson deliveries. • Your preparation marks a teacher who is passionate about teaching and learning. • Your content knowledge was appropriate for the lesson. • You checked for understanding using open-ended questions. • Your instructional strategies were relevant to achieving the objective. • You built the lesson on prior knowledge. • You communicated and presented material clearly.
Knowledge	**Needs Attention/Unsatisfactory**
	• The lesson was brief. • The lesson could have been enhanced by linking the day's activities to lessons learned on previous days. • The lesson plan did not contain enough components to adequately address the curriculum. • Give attention to the lesson opening, one that states what is about to happen and why. • Give attention to providing a lesson closure. • The main concern is always, are students learning?
Lesson Plans	**Excellent/Satisfactory**
	• You employed an opening activity that was purposeful. • During the opening, you communicated the scope and sequence of the content to be covered. • The opening activity established a solid foundation for new information and supported the lesson's goals. • You started by linking the lesson to yesterday's lesson. • You constructed the lesson in a manner that made the content relevant to the interests of this grade level.

Useful Comments 117

- You utilized a variety of questioning techniques to ascertain learning.
- You conducted a discussion about the content being taught.
- You taught to the objectives.
- You made maximum use of instructional resources, materials, and time.
- You engaged students in hands-on activities to aid in their understanding and mastery.
- You honored the time frame for the lesson plan.
- The lesson appealed to students and was appropriate for the curriculum and aligned to the goals of the lesson.
- The closure clearly reviewed the lesson objectives and learning tasks.

Lesson Plans   **Needs Attention/Unsatisfactory**

- Be sure to open with a statement about the lesson.
- The activities planned were not congruent with the stated objectives.
- Learning materials were not handy/ready for use.
- Insufficient time was left for lesson closure.
- A good lesson should end with a closure.
- Please make sure your lessons have an appropriate opening and closing.
- Close with an overview of the next day's lesson.
- Always plan your work and work your plan.

Organization   **Excellent/Satisfactory**

- Plans showed evidence of preparation of a variety of interactive tasks that richly complemented the content.
- Activities were planned that related to students' knowledge base, interests, and life experiences.
- You utilized every minute of available class time.
- Transitions between tasks were smooth and well thought out.
- You provided timely feedback.
- You monitored students' progress throughout the lesson.
- You kept the plan congruent with the stated objectives.
- Strategies geared toward engaging all students in the lesson activities were utilized.

Organization   **Needs Attention/Unsatisfactory**

- In the future, model sample experiments to illustrate expected outcomes.
- Better organization is needed ahead of time to avoid class disruption.
- The lesson plan was overly ambitious.
- Instructional time must be well managed.
- Insufficient time was allowed for group tasks to be completed.
- Insufficient time was allowed for students to practice what they had been taught.
- A focus on best practices was not in evidence.

Development	**Excellent/Satisfactory**
	• You utilized new skills to encourage students to actively participate.
• You utilized new technology as an effective teaching method.
• You demonstrated knowledge of best practices.
• You provided excellent feedback on the use of new skills.
• Students were challenged to think and to problem solve using new skills.
• You used effective teaching practices learned during a seminar.
• You planned creative and productive group activities based on staff development training.
Development	**Needs Attention/Unsatisfactory**
	• The lesson content lacked some/all elements related to staff development training.
• You failed to utilize instruction methodologies recommended in staff training sessions.
• Be more mindful of information provided during training about this grade/age level.
• Consider using staff development training to provide more variety in the learning experiences.
• The lesson did not have the depth and breadth required to meet recommendations made during staff training.
• The planned activities were not appropriate for the current developmental goals.

Table 14.3.   Classroom Management

Supervision	**Excellent/Satisfactory**
	• Instruction was provided in a clear manner and was interesting, which prevented behavioral issues.
• You asked many questions to gauge comprehension.
• You appeared confident and poised.
• Because you planned such an interesting and informative lesson, students were attentive and well behaved.
• You conducted a meaningful class discussion on narratives that kept students engaged.
• You scanned the room often.
• You frequently circulated throughout the room.
Supervision	**Needs Attention/Unsatisfactory**
	• Circulate more throughout the classroom to ensure participation.
• I do not feel that you exhibited a take-charge attitude.
• Scan the room more often.
• Remember when you set your instructional groups to identify ways to monitor the work of all students.
• Work on disciplinary techniques for poor behavior.
• Be aware of behavioral problems as they start, to avoid having them spin out of control.

Communication	**Excellent/Satisfactory**

• You used appropriate facial and physical behaviors, gestures, and language.
• You exhibited appropriate confidence and poise.
• This was an impressive undertaking, and you did a great job.
• You clearly communicated expectations for learning.
• You opened with a relevant anticipatory activity that set the tone for lesson success.
• You stressed the important points.
• Sharing life experiences related to the subject matter kept students interested and on task.
• You utilized a variety of questioning techniques.
• You provided clarification and praise when needed.

Communication	**Needs Attention/Unsatisfactory**

• Remember to sprinkle more praise throughout your lesson.
• Give attention to a lesson opening that states what is about to happen and why.
• Scan the room periodically for raised hands.
• Define key terms on posters/reference sheets.
• The material's size appeared to be too small for all students to adequately see.
• Give attention to providing a lesson closure.
• Align lesson closure to the objectives.
• As you monitor seat work, offer encouragement.

Behavior	**Excellent/Satisfactory**

• You encouraged students by continuously modeling expectations.
• Ongoing feedback was offered to maintain focused participation.
• You demonstrated the ability to motivate students.
• Positive instructional strategies were employed to promote learning.
• Students were privileged to have you provide instruction in such an imaginative, innovative, and competent way.
• I observed fairness and patience toward all students.

Behavior	**Needs Attention/Unsatisfactory**

• Consistently capture and maintain students' attentive behaviors.
• Students were not as cooperative as they should have been.
• Consistently enforce the classroom code of conduct.
• Eliminate choral responses.
• Require students to raise their hands and wait to be called on before speaking.
• Require students to remain in their seats unless the lesson calls for other activity.
• Practice assertiveness.
• It is important to anticipate and avoid off-task behavior.
• Work on requiring students to acknowledge and self-correct unproductive behaviors.

	• Know the classroom code of conduct. • Consistently enforce the code of conduct.
Environment	**Excellent/Satisfactory**
	• You provided a nurturing and supportive atmosphere for learning. • The classroom arrangement was appropriate for this type of instruction. • The classroom was rearranged in a way that fit the day's activities. • You managed classroom routines and procedures without loss of instructional time. • You created and maintained a classroom environment that was rich in educational opportunities for all students.
Environment	**Needs Attention/Unsatisfactory**
	• Identify a more structured way to collect finished work. • Have students remain seated unless/until there is a need for them to move. • Establish the rules of engagement for hands-on lessons. • Identify a different process for rearranging the classroom for new activities. • Identify ways to manage routines and procedures to avoid loss of instructional time.

Table 14.4. Teaching with Rigor

Instruction	**Excellent/Satisfactory**
	• You communicated expectations. • You began the lesson with a warm-up activity related to prior learning. • You asked probing questions. • You entertained questions. • You provided precise explanations. • Opportunities were provided for students to apply newly acquired knowledge.
Instruction	**Needs Attention/Unsatisfactory**
	• Ensure that information on the board/slides is visible to all students. • Use a pointer or yardstick when pointing out and/or clarifying information. • At the beginning of the lesson, write the objectives on the board. • Have students repeat the objectives. • Ask students to define key components of the lesson plan. • Probe students' knowledge with leading questions.
Feedback	**Excellent/Satisfactory**
	• You monitored student attentiveness and comprehension throughout. • You provided praise that encouraged continuous engagement. • You provided individual attention when and where needed.

Useful Comments

Feedback	• You praised students for their efforts and accomplishments. • You allowed students to reinforce their knowledge by calling on them for additional explanations. • You rephrased where needed to promote understanding.
Feedback	**Needs Attention/Unsatisfactory** • A variety of hands-on/more interactive assignments will greatly enhance student engagement. • Students might benefit from seeing their work posted. • Work on relating lesson content to previous/future learning. • The questions posed were not thought provoking. • Allow students to participate more. • Be open to new ideas/perspectives offered by students.
Engagement	**Excellent/Satisfactory** • You started the lesson with a warm-up. • You used visuals to review/determine levels of retained knowledge. • You called students by name. • You asked probing questions. • Each student presented his/her finished work to the class. • You led the lesson by having students repeat after you. • The lesson content was related to students' experiences. • You closed the lesson by allowing students to share what they had learned with a partner.
Engagement	**Needs Attention/Unsatisfactory** • Do allow for more opportunities for engagement. • Group assignments can connect students to their supportive peers. • When you ask questions, strive for more meaningful answers. • Use a variety of materials/approaches to keep students' attention. • Check in occasionally to ensure that all students are on track. • Give equal attention to all group members. • Incorporate the use of technology in less-confusing ways.
Reflective Teaching	**Excellent/Satisfactory** • You are a natural in the classroom. • You planned comprehensively. • The supplemental materials greatly enhanced students' grasp of the lesson. • Your reflective teaching style allows you to think through your teaching practices. • Your reflective teaching method allows you to analyze how to target better learning outcomes. • The use of various methods signaled that you planned for the spectrum of learners.
Reflective Teaching	**Needs Attention/Unsatisfactory** • Rather than telling students what you want them to do, demonstrate/model expectations. • Prepare better teaching aids.

- Prepare a more comprehensive lesson plan.
- Be mindful of the need to provide background information for the lesson.
- Prepare in a way that provides students with all the relevant details.
- Select teaching aids that are child centered and relevant to the objective.
- Prepare a closure that sums up the lesson's points.

Table 14.5. Teamsmanship/Spirit of Cooperation

Rapport with Students	Excellent/Satisfactory
	• You made personal connections with your students. • You maintained a positive rapport with students. • You provided help, support, and encouragement to all learners. • You provided individual attention where needed. • Your dedication to excellence and concern for students was felt. • Your voice was strong. • Students could easily see and hear you throughout the class. • You self-corrected your mistake. • You used a caring tone and offered words of encouragement. • You called on volunteers and nonvolunteers alike. • You used guided practice to illustrate expectations.
Rapport with Students	Needs Attention/Unsatisfactory
	• Unfortunately, I didn't observe a lot of connection/rapport. • Utilize a variety of methods to ensure that all students are engaged. • Encourage students to build rapport with you so they feel comfortable asking for assistance. • I would like to see you circulate around the classroom more and call on more students. • All students need to be given the opportunity to interact with you. • The atmosphere in the classroom was more one of a disciplinary leader rather than one who connects with students. • Build an environment that enables mutual respect.
Rapport with Parents	Excellent/Satisfactory
	• Your lesson was relevant to the home lives/personal experiences of students. • The lesson promoted student and parental involvement. • You connected class activities to students' daily lives and the lives of their parents. • You encouraged students to speak to their parents about activities related to the lesson. • The lesson reinforced skills through probing questions that linked the lesson plan to everyday activities. • Your lesson content was related to students' personal interests.

Useful Comments

Rapport with Parents
Needs Attention/Unsatisfactory

- I would like to see you utilize more real-world examples in the lessons.
- Encourage students to think about their lives outside of school when probing for comprehension.
- Consider assigning homework that encourages students to read aloud to a sibling or a parent.
- Consider assigning homework that requires hands-on activities.
- Provide better updates to parents about classroom activities.

Respect for Administration
Excellent/Satisfactory

- You related the lesson to the activities performed by principals/teachers/school staff.
- You demonstrated your clear regard for everyone who works at the school.
- You presented a lesson based on activities performed by school staff.
- You supported verbal direction using visual aids similar to equipment used in the school.
- You actively showed respect/support for school administration/staff.

Respect for Administration
Needs Attention/Unsatisfactory

- When students disrespect another teacher, model your regard for fellow professionals.
- When students shared negative information about other teachers, you responded in an unprofessional manner.
- You encouraged disrespect for your peers.
- Your support of peers/school staff was less than exemplary.
- Your comments about peers/school staff were inappropriate.

Respect for Diversity
Excellent/Satisfactory

- You seem to have a grasp of how each of your students learns best.
- You showed respect and fairness for all students.
- All students were encouraged to become active learners.
- Teaching methods were adjusted as needed to serve a diverse group of students.
- You demonstrated a high degree of respect for diverse perspectives.
- The activities fit the needs of a diverse group of students.
- You demonstrated respect for different perspectives in the lesson's delivery.
- You used appropriate facial and physical behaviors, gestures, and language while working with students from a variety of backgrounds.

	• You exhibited appropriate confidence and poise in working with students from a variety of backgrounds.
Respect for Diversity	**Needs Attention/Unsatisfactory**
	• Do be aware of gender differences in some cultures. • Maintain an atmosphere of mutual respect. • Call on girls even if they don't volunteer to answer a question. • The examples you shared didn't connect well with these students. • Your questions did not display sensitivity to students' personal backgrounds. • Your questions/lesson did not display respect for cultural diversity. • Students cannot respond to situations they have not experienced themselves.

Table 14.6.   Administrative Duties

Record Keeping	**Excellent/Satisfactory**
	• Your discussion/activities allowed for individual assessment. • I saw close monitoring and good lesson pacing. • The assignment added to students' folders created a historical record of their progress. • The self-assessment opportunity allowed students to reflect on their progress. • You used appropriate methods to track student progress.
Record Keeping	**Needs Attention/Unsatisfactory**
	• Supplemental materials, such as props, charts, graphic organizers, and/or other teaching aids, would provide opportunities to track student progress. • Ask questions to ensure comprehension. • Always begin class with material related to prior lessons. • Compile your attendance records for future mixed-grade units to reduce the time spent on this duty. • Select activities that have specific goals to enable individual student assessment.
Paraprofessional Management	**Excellent/Satisfactory**
	• The list of duties and responsibilities provided to the paraprofessional was comprehensive and detailed. • Having the paraprofessional take over routine tasks freed you for short interactions with individual students/other duties. • Your approach to guiding the paraprofessional was professional and collegial. • Mutual respect between you and the paraprofessional was modeled.

- Lesson plans were provided to the paraprofessional ahead of time.
- You defined the lesson objectives in detail so the paraprofessional's support was always in sync with the final goals.
- You gave clear directions and explanations to the paraprofessional.

Paraprofessional Management — Needs Attention/Unsatisfactory

- Instructional time could have been better managed by providing the paraprofessional with materials/lesson plans ahead of time.
- Providing instructions to the paraprofessional in the moment disrupts the flow of learning.
- Since materials were not provided to the paraprofessional ahead of time, she/he was unable to function in the most effective manner.
- Treat the paraprofessional in a way that models the respect students should hold for her/him.
- Hand off more of the daily tasks to the paraprofessional to free up your time for teaching. Allow the paraprofessional to assist students to give all learners the chance to advance.

Grading System — Excellent/Satisfactory

- You asked students to look at their score from the prior day.
- You provided clear and concise directions throughout the lesson.
- You rewarded student efforts with specific marks.
- Students were given the opportunity to self-assess.
- At the end of the lesson, the performance chart was reviewed.
- Grading feedback was immediate.
- Grading method was fair and transparent.
- An appropriate data sheet was used to document learning.
- Learning was assessed via observation/written answers.

Grading System — Needs Attention/Unsatisfactory

- Clearly explain the lesson objectives/learning tasks.
- Circulate throughout the room to monitor students' work.
- Take teaching activities through to a logical conclusion and evaluate outcomes.
- Plan a lesson that produces measurable outcomes.
- The final product was not collected.
- Challenge students to understand the process by which answers are reached.
- Compile tangible results to track performance and set grades.

Rules and Regulations — Excellent/Satisfactory

- You wrote a plan that was clearly aligned to the mandates associated with this grade level.
- The lesson challenged students to think critically.

	• By modeling the activity, you ensured that the materials would be used in a safe manner. • The class responded well to the code of conduct. • You prepared a variety of appropriate supplemental materials to meet educational mandates. • You utilized varied teaching strategies to achieve the expected academic advancement. • You provided clear directions and relevant examples.
Rules and Regulations	**Needs Attention/Unsatisfactory** • The supplemental materials did not meet curricular mandates. • The lesson fell short of meeting the instructional objective. • The lesson fell short in meeting educational mandates. • A broader approach in the reference materials/lesson plan is needed to meet educational goals. • The opening activity did not relate well to the lesson. • A concrete framework for the lesson was not provided. • Work on maintaining a focus on the lesson objective. • The examples failed to support mandates.

Table 14.7.   Instruction

Assessment	**Excellent/Satisfactory** • You posed questions that required open-ended thinking to allow students to demonstrate their level of learning. • You encouraged students to participate actively during the delivery of the lesson. • You provided help and support to all learners. • The lesson plan provided measurable, evidence-based results. • You utilized hands-on instructional materials that engaged students mentally and physically. • You continuously monitored students' progress and made adjustments when necessary. • Your attention to detail and organizational skills resulted in quality assessments.
Assessment	**Needs Attention/Unsatisfactory** • Students were given little time to respond to questions. • Students' comments were cut off. • The activities provided little opportunity to assess individual learning. • The task provided little opportunity to signal when adjustments should be made. • Students were not encouraged to participate in the lesson. • Questions were not directed to students. • Students raised their hands but were not called on frequently. • Little monitoring of student comprehension occurred.

Technology	**Excellent/Satisfactory**
	• You demonstrated proficient use of technology.
• You infused technology into the lesson presentation.
• You encouraged students to share ideas and thoughts by posting on the school's social media.
• You incorporated a short video to provide lesson clarity.
• You used an interactive digital activity to pique interest.
• You infused technology in the support materials.
• You infused technology into the students' assignment.
• You used appropriate technology to stimulate interest.
• The PowerPoint presentation was on target for learning objectives.
Technology	**Needs Attention/Unsatisfactory**
	• Test devices/programs ahead of time.
• Always have a backup plan for alternate activities in cases when technology fails.
• Please familiarize yourself with the technology you plan to use.
• The failure of a device shouldn't take the entire lesson off track.
• Design digital elements that are congruent with the objectives of the lesson.
• The technology selected did not enhance understanding.
• The technology selected did not provide enrichment.
Cocurricular Activities	**Excellent/Satisfactory**
	• The activities related to cocurricular activities tied to the lesson.
• The activities related to the students' cocurricular interests.
• Your instructional method stimulated interest through cocurricular activities.
• You kept the lesson moving by replicating cocurricular-style activities in class.
• You provided a variety of learning experiences by drawing on cocurricular activities.
• You allowed students to think beyond the limits of the textbook by introducing the need for today's lesson in cocurricular activities.
Cocurricular Activities	**Needs Attention/Unsatisfactory**
	• Take care not to allow the focus of the class to wander too far when discussing/utilizing cocurricular activities.
• The activity drawn from a cocurricular component was too complex for this age range.
• Instructional time was not maximized due to the overuse of cocurricular activities.
• The emphasis on cocurricular activities did not meet learning goals.
• The emphasis on cocurricular activities did not meet mandates.

Differentiated Instruction	Excellent/Satisfactory
	• You presented images that were colorful and clear. • The use of proximity teaching encouraged reluctant learners to participate. • You implemented a variety of teaching methods for students with varied learning preferences/challenges. • You enhanced the lesson through various learning aids. • You used a variety of teaching strategies to achieve the lesson objective. • The students engaged in hands-on activities to aid in mastery. • You supported verbal directions with overhead visuals and excellent examples.
Differentiated Instruction	Needs Attention/Unsatisfactory
	• Create extended activities for students who finish early. • Visuals need to be much clearer in terms of demonstrating the lesson's main points. Supplemental materials need to add quality to the lesson. • Supplemental materials need to be more varied. • Provide students with more creative activities. • Assign students more high-interest tasks. • Utilize small groups. • Provide individual instruction to students who are in need.

Table 14.8. Pastoral Duties

Academic Issues	Excellent/Satisfactory
	• You set realistic goals for students and motivated them to reach those goals. • The assistance provided to students demonstrated an understanding of their needs. • You closely monitored student progress during group assignments. • You managed time effectively while counseling individuals. • You ensured that every student was given the same access to the supplementary materials. • You consistently provided all students with an equal opportunity to participate.
Academic Issues	Needs Attention/Unsatisfactory
	• Be aware of the physical difficulties some students have when planning activities. • Promote positive group interactions. • Provide alternate hands-on activities/materials for students who have physical challenges.

- Pair students up during challenging activities so they can work according to what each individual can do.
- Be aware of the special needs associated with vision/hearing impaired students.

Encouragement Excellent/Satisfactory

- You effectively utilized vivid voice inflections to generate excitement.
- You structured a lesson that promoted maximum student involvement.
- You successfully maintained a friendly and pleasant atmosphere.
- The environment you built and maintained encouraged and enhanced self-confidence and self-worth.
- Individuals who struggled were given specific encouragement during the lesson/personal follow-ups.
- You immediately responded to one student's distress.
- You listened to students and responded in a manner that was caring.
- The student in need was referred to the counselor.

Encouragement Needs Attention/Unsatisfactory

- You did not clearly communicate expectations for learning/success.
- You did not engage all learners in activities that were meaningful/creative.
- The lesson plan was too ambitious to garner confidence in students.
- Value the contribution of each student.
- Your patience wore thin.
- Your response to a student in need was below expected levels of support.
- You did not respond to a student in need.

Communication with Others Excellent/Satisfactory

- You used good communication skills with the individuals who were visiting.
- You spoke clearly.
- You exhibited a cooperative and helpful approach with other teachers/visitors.
- You provided individual attention to other teachers/visitors.
- Before class, you engaged with parents/peers/staff.
- You exhibited patience/professionalism/a positive attitude while communicating with others.

Communication with Others Needs Attention/Unsatisfactory

- Your response to comments about another teacher could have been misinterpreted.
- Provide peers with every opportunity to be represented with respect.

- Your response to the parent/peer/staff was inappropriate.
- You undermined your relationship with the parent/peer/staff.
- You did not model appropriate maturity for students.

Extracurricular Participation	Excellent/Satisfactory
	• You wrote a good plan that utilized extracurricular activities/staff. • You called in the leader of an after-school club. • You stimulated learning associated with an extracurricular topic. • A variety of activities were tied to an extracurricular topic. • You planned a lesson that motivated students to participate in the classroom as well as in after-school clubs. • You provided information relating to an extracurricular activity.
Extracurricular Participation	Needs Attention/Unsatisfactory
	• Learn exactly what the after-school clubs do so you will be prepared for questions. • Your response about after-school clubs did not encourage participation in extracurricular activities. • Refrain from expressing adversarial comments that might turn students away from enriching after-school programs.

Table 14.9. Core Behavioral Competencies

Creativity, Adaptability, and Flexibility	Excellent/Satisfactory
	• The materials were highly appropriate/creative in their approach. • You varied teaching strategies as needed to fit the abilities of different students. • You pulled in an array of manipulative and hands-on aids. • Your instructional strategies were unique and engaging. • When difficulties arose, you shifted gears and continued with an effective lesson. • Lots of real-world anecdotes were used to engage students.
Creativity, Adaptability, and Flexibility	Needs Attention/Unsatisfactory
	• Use a variety of strategies, including oral response, written tasks, and hands-on activities. • Offer activities that are hands-on and minds-on. • The manner in which students answered the questions could have been more varied. • Ask more detailed questions about unique lesson elements to better guide students.

Useful Comments

	• Instructional materials were not geared well toward stimulating interest. • Vary the content to demonstrate different elements of the lesson. • The approach to teaching could engage students more creatively.
Decision-Making Skills	**Excellent/Satisfactory** • Your selection of different apps for use during class meets the demands for the highly skilled professional approach required in today's classrooms. • Your students benefit from the effort you put into researching/implementing new resources. • You put a lot of thought into creating a lesson that would meet requirements. • The decisions you made about materials challenged students to perform. • You engaged students in activities that supported lesson mastery.
Decision-Making Skills	**Needs Attention/Unsatisfactory** • Make more appropriate selections for technology. • The approach for poor behaviors needs to be changed. • The homework must be related to the classroom work. • Used a problem-based approach to your teaching methodologies. • The decisions you made about materials did not meet the expected standards. • The activities you chose for this lesson did not achieve mastery. • Spend time researching/implementing new resources for your classroom.
Problem Solving	**Excellent/Satisfactory** • A student's outburst was met with a calm attitude. • When a student lashed out, you did not react to that attack. • You privately spoke to an upset student. • You worked with an upset student to locate a solution. • Changes have been made to eliminate prior issues. • You used assertive discipline strategies to calm the classroom tone. • You redirected off-task behavior.
Problem Solving	**Needs Attention/Unsatisfactory** • You did not monitor students' attentiveness well enough to locate the source of issues. • You responded inappropriately to a challenge. • Your response to a challenge was less than optimal. • Your response to poor behavior was lacking in corrective disciplinary methods. • Clearly indicate the types of behavior that are and are not allowed in your classroom. • Consequences need to be applied for continued disruptions.

Resilience and Tenacity	Excellent/Satisfactory
	• You handled the challenge(s) very well. • With this challenging group of students, you varied your approach to different issues. • You changed methods as the lesson progressed in response to specific difficulties. • The conflicts that arose were corrected with care. • You persisted in a patient and nurturing approach. • You changed tactics until you found the method that resolved the difficulty. • Your response to classroom issues was accurate and timely. • You corrected students' behaviors immediately. • You exhibited a dedication to resolving issues.
Resilience and Tenacity	Needs Attention/Unsatisfactory
	• Vary the methods of instruction to promote interest and reduce disruptions. • Your caring and encouraging tone began to sound frustrated. • Individual attention was not provided every time it was needed. • You stopped providing support when certain students continued to struggle. • Persistence is a must. • Support must be continuous.

Table 14.10. Teacher as a Leader

Modeling Lifelong Learning	Excellent/Satisfactory
	• Every step was introduced by your own experiences. • You utilized materials culled from the real world. • You modeled how to use the lesson's content every day. • You encouraged students to engage with information relevant to their world. • You displayed a love of continual learning. • You discussed why an understanding of the lesson's content is important.
Modeling Lifelong Learning	Needs Attention/Unsatisfactory
	• Nothing in this unit was tied to the world outside of the classroom. • You did not share experiences based on your background in this topic. • Promote cognitive thinking throughout the lesson. • Students failed to understand how the curriculum is applicable outside the classroom.

	• By sticking so closely to the textbook, you did not model lifelong learning.
Collaborative Teaching/ Learning	Excellent/Satisfactory
	• The activity helped students connect what they know with the day's lesson. • The small-group activity promoted maximum participation. • The task you assigned allowed for thinking and doing to be shared between students. • You promoted the use/development of cooperative skills. • Students presented their finished work in pairs. • You provided the opportunity for students to help each other. • You placed peer-to-peer assistance in the hands of the students. • You encouraged student self-control while interacting with peers.
Collaborative Teaching/ Learning	Needs Attention/Unsatisfactory
	• Ask students to read their completed answers aloud. • Have students form groups based on their answers to assigned tasks. • Find ways for students to interact with each other. • Find ways for students to help each other excel. • Allow groups enough time to finish the assignment. • Give equal attention to all groups and group members. • Ensure that group assignments require interactions between students.
System Support	Excellent/Satisfactory
	• Learning was made relevant by considering the interests of students in other curricular areas. • You planned a good lesson that reached into other subject areas to support learning. • The materials were borrowed from other classrooms/areas of the school. • Students shared their performance in other subject areas.
System Support	Needs Attention/Unsatisfactory
	• The unit did not integrate the new approach. • Pay attention to new mandates. • You did not integrate the components discussed in the latest recommendations. • Utilize the concrete frameworks developed to improve education along the common themes targeted school wide.
Mentoring	Excellent/Satisfactory
	• You clearly explained how to solve the new teacher's issue. • You provided a copy of your materials to the new teacher.

- Your mentoring assistance was provided quickly and with minimal fuss.
- The teacher you mentor feels confident in your support.
- The lesson allowed for an equal amount of teaching by both instructors.
- The teamwork supported best practices.
- The co-teaching approach ensured learning success.

Mentoring   **Needs Attention/Unsatisfactory**

- You must track all elements involved with the individual you are assisting.
- Keep in mind that [fill in] is not the only area in which to assist.
- The plans/materials you provided to the new teacher were incomplete.
- Work on enhancing the mentor's confidence in your support.
- The first-year teacher was left to his/her own devices while attempting [fill in].

Chapter Fifteen

Performance Tier Words and Phrases

In using the prewritten comments from the previous chapter, you will sometimes wish to make minor adjustments. This ensures that the comments will say exactly what you mean and communicate precisely the message you intend to convey.

The table in this chapter provides you with words and phrases grouped according to their use in each performance tier. Their nuances allow you to locate the exact word you need in a fast and efficient manner.

Table 15.1.

Performance Tier	Words	Phrases
Excellent	• Best	• Great teachers are
	• Captivating	• Settle for nothing less than excellence
	• Commendable	• Prepare the launch pad
	• Comprehensive	• You are making a difference
	• Detailed	• The behavior of a masterful teacher
	• Energetic	• Students are privileged
	• Energizing	• Highly appropriate
	• Enriching	• Your students benefit from
	• Enthusiastic	• You exhibited
	• Excellence	• You owned
	• Exceptional	• From start to finish
	• Impressive	• It was evident that you
	• Masterful	• I imagine that you spend countless hours
	• Passionate	• You tied the lesson into
	• Phenomenal	• I observed a high degree of
	• Specific	• Provided every student with the opportunity to
	• Sterling	
	• Thought-provoking	
	• Tireless	

	• Total	
	• Vivid	
Satisfactory	• Appropriate	• You modeled
	• Better	• I was impressed with how well you
	• Child-centered	handled
	• Clearly	• You delivered
	• Collegial	• You created
	• Competent	• Sound teaching
	• Concrete	• Motivated learners
	• Creative	• Contributed to clarity
	• Credible	• Modeled for students
	• Effective	• Congruent with standards
	• Encouraged	• Sufficient time was allowed
	• Engaging	• You maintained
	• Focused	• Quite fitting
	• Fun	• You came across as
	• Good	• Made learning fun
	• Inspired	• Your preparation marks a teacher who is
	• Interesting	• Relevant to the interests of this grade level
	• Meaningful	• You utilized a variety of
	• Positive	• You made maximum use of
	• Professional	• You engaged students in
	• Proficient	• Your students reap dividends from
	• Quality	• Students were challenged to
	• Relevant	• You used appropriate
	• Respectful	• You exhibited appropriate
	• Sound	• You incorporated
	• Specific	• You infused
	• Success	• Was on target for
	• Targeted	
Needs Improvement	• Always	• Try not to
	• Anticipate	• Work on
	• Avoid	• Less than effective
	• Check	• Ensure that
	• Clarify	• In the future
	• Comprehensive	• Actions that could have added quality
	• Concise	• Strive to
	• Connected	• Students need
	• Consistently	• Adjust your teaching whenever you
	• Enhance	• For the most part lacked
	• Ensure	• Review strategies to use with
	• Frequently	• Consistently reinforce
	• Integrate	• Please show
	• Lacked	• The lesson could have been enhanced by
	• Maintain	• Give attention to
	• Manage	• Utilize a variety of
	• Perform	• Please make sure
	• Precise	• Challenge students to
	• Purposeful	• Be more mindful of
	• Relevant	• Consider using

	• Remember	• Provide more variety in
	• Review	• Remember to
	• Support	• Require students to
	• Utilize	• It is important to anticipate
		• Identify a more structured way to
		• Identify a different process for
		• Always have a backup plan
Unsatisfactory	• Confusing	• The teacher did not
	• Disallowed	• Was not provided in a professional manner
	• Disorganized	• Did not meet mandates
	• Disrespectful	• Did not meet learning goals
	• Distracting	• Demonstrate a positive attitude toward
	• Failed	• Show more enthusiasm for
	• Ignored	• Use an appropriate
	• Incompetent	• The lesson plan did not contain
	• Ineffective	• The main concern is
	• Inefficient	• Did not align with stated objective
	• Insufficient	• Was not handy/ready for use
	• Irrelevant	• Insufficient time was allotted to
	• Lacking	• Overly ambitious
	• Never	• Must be well managed
	• Poor	• A focus on best practices was not in evidence
	• Substandard	
	• Unacceptable	• Did not have depth and breadth
	• Unengaging	• Inappropriate for/unrelated to the goals
	• Uninformative	• I do not feel that you exhibited
	• Uninspiring	• Unfortunately, I didn't observe
	• Unprofessional	• Students need the opportunity to
	• Unrelated	• Provided little opportunity to
	• Weak	• The technology selected did not

WORDS OF PRAISE

Because calling out strengths is as important as calling out weaknesses, this section deals with additional words of praise. Use these to enhance dedication, encourage even higher performance levels, and make the appraisal process a positive event.

- Students learn best by doing, and today's lesson allowed them to actively learn.
- You projected a belief in yourself.
- You projected a belief in the potential of students to achieve the objectives.
- What a pleasure it was to observe a lesson provided with strong methods that inspired students to learn and generated a powerful academic environment.

- You delivered the lesson like a master teacher.
- This observation was so refreshing and rewarding.
- You are an outstanding teacher.
- Keep up the good work.
- It is a pleasure to observe a lesson where students are challenged/allowed to explore.
- You are a master at planning.
- You are a master at conducting hands-on activities that support the lesson objectives.
- You are commended for consistent and successful efforts.
- I look forward to seeing you continue to grow.
- You did an excellent job.
- How fortunate your students are to have you as their teacher.
- You are innately a strong professional.
- I observed exceptional professional practices.
- You are commended for [fill in].
- You demonstrated skill in [fill in].
- You have mastered a variety of teaching techniques.
- I have no doubt that you will continue to grow and expand as a professional.
- Total professionalism was demonstrated as you guided students through this lesson.
- I have no doubt you will continue to strive for ultimate success for your students.
- This class is lucky to have a teacher who leads them with competency, imagination, and enthusiasm.
- Thank you for making learning fun and exciting.
- I thoroughly enjoyed watching you work inside the classroom.
- It was evident that you want to create experiences that will be highly engaging.
- You owned this lesson from beginning to end.
- It was evident that a great deal of thought and preparation went into designing this lesson for success.
- Remember that I am cheering for you and want you to succeed.
- Your energy and enthusiasm for teaching encourages and motivates your students.
- You exhibited excellent teaching habits.
- Continue to seek innovative ways to challenge your students just as you did today.
- You teach students to think.
- You are well on your way to becoming an outstanding teacher.
- The detailed lesson and materials proved your dedication and enhanced students' progress.

- You exemplify professional traits through word and deed.
- You did an excellent job.
- Kudos for a job well done.
- Your excitement and enthusiasm are exactly what is needed in today's classrooms.
- I observed a teacher well on her/his way to becoming a top professional.
- You have a creative and artful teaching style.
- I am proud of the standards you have set for yourself as a teacher.

About the Author

For forty-three years, **Dr. Barbara D. Culp** has dedicated herself to education. After teaching at the elementary and middle school levels, she eventually became the principal of a large elementary school and was selected as Principal of the Year. Recently, she resigned as a part-time clinical supervisor for Brenau University's School of Education to devote more time to her family and tutorial services company. Dr. Culp graduated from Morris Brown College and Atlanta University with a master's degree and an education doctoral degree in administration and supervision. In addition, she graduated from the rigorous, two-year Georgia Superintendent Professional Development Program. She has conducted workshops and training programs on classroom management, differentiated instruction, and other topics of interest to educators.

www.ingramcontent.com/pod-product-compliance
Lightning Source LLC
Chambersburg PA
CBHW021851300426
44115CB00005B/114